PEOPLE THAT DON'T EXIST ARE CITIZENS OF A MADE-UP COUNTRY

By Joe Horgan

PEOPLE THAT DON'T EXIST ARE CITIZENS OF A MADE-UP COUNTRY

Essays on Immigrants, Migrants and Refugees

So we live here, forever taking leave

RAINER MARIA RILKE

First published in 2021
by Black Spring Press Group

Suite 333, 19–21 Crawford Street
Marylebone, London W1H 1PJ
United Kingdom

Typeset by Subash Raghu
Cover design by Edwin Smet
Painting by Bernard Canavan

ISBN 978-1-913606-07-7

BLACKSPRINGPRESSGROUP.COM

To my brother, David

CONTENTS

FOREWORD

This book was written in the hills of rural Cork looking down on Dan and Margaret Murphy's farm. A short way along the lane from here, between two derelict outbuildings, a break in the trees gives a framed vista of the other side of the valley. In the distance the traffic of the main Cork road and, in the rain, vast flocks of boisterous crows. An old map of this area shows that there were once twelve dwellings in the yard at the top of this lane. There is now just one, solitary, house. It is a fairly sure bet, this being Ireland, that some of the people from those vanished dwellings went on to become immigrants, migrants, economic refugees.

On the walls of an Irish social club in England there is a painted version of this scene. The boreen winds off above the chairs, the artist's skill giving it the perspective of distance, and hay is cocked in the fields. Whitewashed cottages dot the scene and at red half-doors men and women lean out. At a table beneath I sit with my mother and father as they talk and drink. The floor is sticky and on a Saturday night here, or a Sunday afternoon, big-handed men dance with their women and they dance their way back home. Outside are the streets of an English city but inside are the immigrants and it is a different place.

My parents came to England from Cork in 1954 from an Ireland with little work and few prospects for a couple who wanted to start a family and build a life. Prior to emigrating, their knowledge of Britain was scant but newspapers, cinema and word of mouth all spoke of a land with employment opportunities aplenty. It was not, after all, as if emigration was a radical option for the kind of Ireland they lived in or the kind of Irish they were. Whatever, though, about the ubiquity of their choice, the emotional impact of leaving home was not lessened. My mother recounts that for the first six months she hardly left her rooms and that even the simple height of the buildings disturbed her. The city they came to was purely a matter of chance. Manchester, Sheffield, Glasgow, London, were all places of work, all cities of immigration, but in the end, for no identifiable reason they can recall, they went to Birmingham and stayed there for over forty years. So, in the English Midlands, far from their Irish beginnings and the imaginings of their early lives, they had a family in a city they had chosen at random the way some people might make a choice by sticking a pin in a piece of paper.

This is based on a singular, personal story, albeit that the sheer number of Irish immigrants to Britain makes any accounting of even that experience a shared one. More importantly, though, is that a family story can be an insight into something that is more than ever a burning social issue: the question of immigration, of migration, of refugees. At any time during the writing of this I could have stopped and pinpointed a report about migrants in the Mediterranean.

Migrants ashore or migrants drowned. It remains the story of our time, whether it be through Trump's Wall, Brexit's psychological one, or orange-bodied people bobbing in the water.

I'm from inner-city Britain and my voice and my vowels, perhaps my face, betray only that. But in looking for the bogeyman immigrant of tabloid imaginings I didn't have to look far. I just looked to the people I'd grown up with. I just looked at those sitting next to me in the living room.

ALAN KURDÎ

I was in a car driving alongside the Atlantic, looking out at the sea, and on the radio there were voices discussing the death of a three-year-old boy called Alan Kurdî. More accurately they were discussing the photograph of his little body, face down in the sand, the waves lapping around him. They were discussing the image of Alan Kurdî. Not Alan Kurdî himself, but the photograph of Alan Kurdî. One of the voices, these disembodied car radio voices, even talked about the ethics of the photograph on the front of newspapers, being shown around the world, as if the affront was not Alan Kurdî's death but the photograph of his death. Either way it was clear that Alan Kurdî was a photograph now. He wasn't a three-year-old boy. He wasn't a drowned, sodden, three-year-old boy. He wasn't a person. He was a photograph. He wasn't even a migrant. He wasn't even a refugee.

1

He wasn't a displaced person. He wasn't a child. He was a photograph.

In the car beside me, it just so happened, was my father. Sometime in the middle of the 1950s, in his mid-twenties, my father grew tired. By his own recounting he grew weary of a society where the few jobs that existed were given out on the basis of a nod and a wink. He didn't want that. He didn't want, he said, to spend his young years waiting in line. He didn't want to realise too late that the future was going on somewhere else. He didn't want to have to accept the so very little that was on offer. He didn't want to have to be so grateful. So he got on a boat. He got on a boat and he left County Cork and he went across the Irish Sea to Britain. Alongside him, looking out from the railings of that boat, watching the lights of Cork harbour recede, was the woman who would go on to be my mother. She was eighteen and leaving Ireland for the first time. I can see her now as I look in the car mirror. I can see her sitting there in the back seat. She was eighteen years of age and going across the Irish Sea to Britain. Across the cold expanse. Across the water.

I have a picture of her from around that time. She has long, curling black hair and a nearly ankle-length skirt. It's a photograph so it's not her exactly but you can still see her. You can see her eyes and her skin and that long, curling black hair. In the rear-view mirror I can see her now, the same woman some fifty-odd years on. I can see her eyes and her skin and her shorter, still dark, hair. She's aged well. The lines around her eyes few, the greying at the sides little. She's nearly six decades and six children on from the young woman in the photograph but it is still her. She's still there. Six decades on from getting off the boat. She's still in the photograph too.

A three-year-old has lungs that contain roughly the same 300 million air sacs as an adult. They will be smaller, of course, but the child's lungs have attained much of their final structure. They will fill and drown in water quickly. We drown within a matter of minutes. Alan Kurdî, three years of age, drowned in a short space of time. Off the boat and into the sea. Off the migrant boat and into the Mediterranean. Off the refugee boat and into the water. Off the immigrant boat and into the cold and the dark and the wet and into death. The death of a three-year-old boy. This death was never disputed. This death was not questioned, at least, that is, in terms of its veracity. He was dead. The photograph of Alan Kurdî, though, was debated. The photograph of the dead three-year-old boy. The photograph was disputed. They are talking about it now on the radio and I'm no longer looking in the rear-view mirror and we have parked up by the Atlantic and we are all looking out at the sea. Around the same time as my mother and father went across the Irish Sea, my uncle, my mother's brother, went the other way, out there across the Atlantic. He went too. From Cork to New York. The Irish on the move. Thousands sailing.

When the dead Alan Kurdî became a photograph there were those for whom the photograph became the point. It was as if a response to human death had to be within these parameters. In many ways it did. The dead Alan Kurdî became the living example of migrant reality. His image was used again and again to show the true, shocking awfulness of what was happening out there amongst the dark waves. When Alan Kurdî washed ashore he became, to those of us who didn't know him and didn't know his family, the boy in the photograph. He became the photograph. Yet, there were those who attacked a 'self-satisfied feeling of sadness among Western observers'[1] as a way of dismissing a human response to that very photograph. A human response to a human death. At a remove, yes. Because of a photograph, yes. But a human response nonetheless. Instead they said the photograph was a 'snuff photo for progressives.'[2]

---

[1] Brendan O'Neill, *The Spectator*, 3rd September 2015.
[2] Ibid.

In this way compassion was a falsehood. In this way those who wanted to oppose sympathy towards refugees or migrants or immigrants were somehow suggesting that being moved by his dead body was dishonest. In this way those who did not wish for us to think of migrants as human beings used the remove of a photograph to suggest those appalled by Alan Kurdî's death were moved by a mere photograph. If Alan Kurdî had already been reduced, not just by his death but by his status as a migrant, even by our own response, to merely a photograph, there were those who wanted to deny him even that.

When my mother had been in Britain for around a decade she went home to bury her father. She had in her arms her fifth child, just a few months old. Beside the ceaseless Atlantic I can see her now talking to my father. I can see her face. I can see her skin, her living, breathing body. She looks out for a moment at the sea and my father looks too but they have had six children and a life in inner-city England and introspection does not come easily, even now, when there was never room for it before. They begin talking some more. I could reach out right now and touch her skin. I could hold her hand. I could hold her tightly. I must have held on to her tightly when we crossed the Irish Sea, but as a babe in arms I remember less of that, even, than say, a three-year-old would. I do wonder, though, as she crossed that dark Irish Sea, going home for a burial, did those looking on see a young woman and a baby? And when she first travelled out the other way, when she first looked back at the brave, receding lights, did those looking on see a young, hopeful, scared, woman? Did they see a young woman and a young man standing by the railings? And if in their minds they took a picture and kept it did they call it 'young woman on a boat'? Or 'young woman holding a baby on the Irish Sea'? Or did they not see a young woman at all? Did they not see her black, curling hair and her eyes, her skin? Did they not see that? Did they see instead, before them, in their mind's eye, in the picture their memory kept, an emigrant, an immigrant, a migrant, an economic refugee? Even in the picture?

SEAN O'RIORDAN

My mother always told us that when she first arrived in England she was frightened of the buildings. She was frightened of the size of them, the height of them. She was scared of the way they towered above her. She had never experienced that in Cork. There weren't as many high buildings. They didn't loom so large. They didn't lean in so much. They didn't crowd. She didn't feel, as she felt now in the industrial city, that she lived in the space between them. The space between the buildings. We teased her about that. Oh, look mother, a scary house. Mum, I think that building is looking at you. She could recall it, though, as a real thing. The dislocation of emigration not as an academic construct but as a bricks-and-mortar reality. As a fear.

The reality of immigrant life was and usually still is, inner city life. The reality of immigrant life was long, snaking rows of terraced houses. The reality of immigrant life was the built context. The migrant, the immigrant, the economic refugee is first and foremost a resident of the most intense physical environment the country has to offer. The terraced houses going on and on. The sheer brick and concrete fact of the immigrant life. The city at its most city. Is it any wonder then, and I think she'll represent, I think she can step out of the singular, that she felt first and most intensely the buildings. That the first shock she encountered was the existence of the city itself. The unavoidable immanence of the physical city. The first stage of emigration, some have written, is the idea of it, the decision, the plan. This is wrong. The first stage of emigration is the physical shock of being somewhere else.

The boat is the beginning of this. The metal nausea of the rails above the waves, the crossing. But the boat is temporary. The boat is moving. The boat is always leaving and she is leaving on it. An actual, corporeal leaving. The idea of it is nothing in comparison to this and to even include that is to misunder-stand migration. The decision to emigrate, to become a migrant, is a myth. There is no decision. Emigration is not an idea. It is not an abstract. To suggest otherwise is to paint a picture of people discussing options over coffee and quietly debating which offer to take up. Which of these brochures do you like best? I like the look of this place. I've always fancied going there. I suppose, though, thinking about it, we could stay. We could stay put. Shall we? Stay here and have nothing? It is one of our options. We could. Stay. But. Which of these boats do you think looks most reliable? I asked my father, who did not face barbed wire or people-smugglers or a wall, how did we end up here? Why this city? No reason, he said. No particular rea-son I can recall. It was about work and there was no work in Ireland and in England there was work everywhere. No reason, though, as to where. No reason here and not there. No reason there and not here. It was like sticking a pin in a map. We were leaving and then we left. We were emigrating and then we emigrated. We were emigrating and then we were immigrants. We got on the boat and we went. There was no idea. There was no excited discussion. It's not a decision you make. It's not a decision people like us make. It is just something we do. Emigrating from Ireland wasn't about decisions. It was about being born in that house to those people.

The tight, part-of-each-other terraced houses, going on and on. The concrete intensity of the lived place. The council house with a long garden for the children and a bedroom for the boys and a bedroom for the girls. She doesn't know and doesn't realise for a long time the disconnect there is between this place and the rest of the country she is now in. So lost is she in her own dislocation, oh, mom, look that chimney is coming for us, that she is unaware of the disconnect within the country itself, the city. The host population. Many years later one of her children hears it, though, and realises how much they always knew it. In the fevered days after the

Brexit vote, in the undercurrents becoming waves, he happens to be in the company of an Englishwoman from the shires. She is shocked by Brexit. She is appalled by what it appears to say about her country and about her fellow English. They walk down the city street, the inner-city, multicultural street, the stresses and strains and shares of that place. Oh, how wonderful it is, she suddenly says, to see people wearing their traditional costumes. The disconnect. He feels as if he is in the company of a tourist, somebody visiting the streets, the physical, most representative, most peopled, streets of their own country. And to the tourist some of the people there, some of the people on the immigrant-rich streets are not wearing clothes, but costumes. This is the place they live in. This is the invisible world they get off the boat and move into.

The column writers and the column readers will have plenty to say about the young immigrant woman, there she is, looking up at the buildings, plenty of judgements to pass. But she has no idea how little they know of where she is. She is dislocated inside the disconnect and is trying to find her way.

Four out of every five children that were born in Ireland between 1931 and 1941 emigrated in the 1950s.[3] Four out of five. By the 1950s those children had become part of one of the biggest mass movements of people since the Second World War. Four out of five of them getting on boats and going into the cold sea, going across the dark, cold water. To respond as if this was a matter of choice is to react as if it is a story about modes of transport. It is to look now at Syrians, Afghanis, and Libyans floating in sinking orange jackets on the Mediterranean and not to wonder how bad things on dry land must be to make that a preferable alternative. The Irish, of course, were not fleeing civil war or conflict or governmental persecution or the collapse of a State. They were not fleeing death. They

---

[3]   J.J. Lee, *Ireland, 1912–1985: Politics and Society* (CUP, 2010).

were merely fleeing poverty. They were only, to use contemporary parlance, only, only, economic refugees. Because poverty, of course, as we all know, can all empirically confirm, is not political. It is a simple state of affairs. It merely is. Poverty is the weather. It just happens. And man has no impact upon the weather, does he? Between 1945 and 1960 over 500,000 people emigrated from Ireland.[4] Over 500,000 people became immigrants. Over 500,000 of them became migrants. Over half a million. Three out of four of these went across the Irish Sea to Britain. They got on a boat. They got on the boat and some of them must have seen the young woman standing at the railings watching the brave lights of Cork, the rural electrification poles her future husband had once worked on, the lights of Ireland receding into the dark. Half a million people. In one decade, the 1950s, Ireland lost 16% of its population.[5] All of them on the move.

---

[4]   Irial Glynn, *Irish Emigration History* (UCC, 2012).
[5]   Ibid.

All of them crossing the sea. All of them with the feeling that leaving was better than staying. All of them knowing there was no choice.

Of course, there is always a context to people getting on boats, always a reason for why people are floating on the sea. It was not, in the Irish context, guns, bombs, persecution and people traffickers. But there was a context all the same. As the poet Sean O'Riordan wrote on the eve of his sister's emigration in 1949, 'the child is going to England tomorrow. The poor girl. And the bishops and the doctors and the professors and the motor car salesmen are staying at home.'[6]

Yet, for all that the immigrant, the migrant, the refugee, is housed in the most concrete, the most thorough, representation of the urban, the city, in one way she isn't there at all. In one way she never gets off the boat. She is always on it, always out there in the middle of the black-on-blue sea. She never gets off, she never disembarks. She

6   J.J. Lee, ibid.

never stops being on it. The boat is always there and she is always on the boat and she is always leaving. To leave the boat behind, to get off and never look back, to turn down a side street and disappear into the vast, anonymous embrace of the city and the close, tight streets, is to admit to leaving. To let the city have you. It is to have departed. It is to accept emigration. It is to confirm yourself as an immigrant, a migrant, a refugee. It is to admit you will never go back, never go home. To become that and nothing else. So, she never gets off the boat. She is still at the railing looking back. She is still out there as the endless waves go past. The emigrant, the immigrant, the migrant, the refugee. She is as real as you and I. The same skin and the same bones. I have held her hand and held on to her tightly with the sea beneath us. She is not an image or a picture. Not a ghostly woman against a ghostly ship's railing. She is you and I, born in that house to those people. She is out there on the boat and she always will be.

GERRY ADAMS

My mother used to laugh at the English. She didn't do this in a look-at-their-strange-habits kind of way. She wasn't accusing the host nation. She wasn't bewildered by their never going to Mass or by the fact that their grown children never seemed to visit. She wasn't taking advantage of a lazy Irish-English hostility in order to take comfort in prejudice. She wasn't sitting in a house on an English street, so many physical and imaginative miles away from where she began, obsessing about how different the city was. She was too busy for that, too busy finding her feet and staying upright, too busy getting married, too busy having six kids. She was too busy being a Home Help, cleaning elderly English people's homes, to have time to reflect upon the intricacies of English national characteristics or the social differences between English and Irish life. She forgot, as she went through the hours of the day, that the old man in the chair was English or the woman at the door saying goodbye was English too. She didn't have space to acknowledge nationality in every little thing she did. She didn't go into an English shop or buy an English paper or walk the kids to English school. As time went on, as life, predictably, insisted on being lived, she did not respond by insisting each minute was an English minute, each day an English one. The immigrant's obsessions aren't those obsessions. No, she didn't laugh at the English because she was obsessed with them in any way at all. She laughed at the English because they were obsessed with her.

There was an elderly woman whose house my mother cleaned. There wasn't much cleaning because the woman lived alone, my mother said. There wasn't much cleaning because no one ever came to see her. The house was always unchanged. Week after week, she said, the rooms were the same. Nothing was ever moved, nothing. The rooms were always as they were, just the dust, the dust needing chasing away. She watched me, my mother said, she stood in the doorway and watched everything I ever did. She watched me as if she'd never seen an Irishwoman before, like I was something exotic, something unusual, and outside on the street Irish people walking by day after day, all over the city. On every street of the city. Immigrants everywhere. Yet, the English were fascinated by me. She never stopped watching me. Of course, I should say here, my mother knew. The immigrant knows. The migrant and the asylum seeker and the refugee know. Of course they do. They know that a hundred lurid headlines mean they're being watched. They're being watched because the likelihood is that they're thieves. How could they not know that? The old woman watched my mother to make sure she wasn't stealing anything. In the eyes of the onlooker the immigrant never stops being an immigrant. They never stop being from somewhere else, somewhere left. Even when they've stopped being from there, haven't been home in decades, have children with local lives and local accents who don't even know what that left home looks like or smells like or sounds like, even then, they never stop being from there.

There was the woman living on the same street who called her aside one time, my mother taken aback by this sudden intimacy, to tell her she knew my mother hadn't killed those soldiers. She knew she wasn't in the IRA. Absolved, my mother forgot to mention that having six children would have left her very little time to be an active terrorist. On another occasion a man, jokingly perhaps, asked her if she could get a message to Gerry Adams. Indistinguishable in any way, on account of her skin colour, from what was deemed to be the typical idea of an English-woman my mother admitted to trying not to speak after certain IRA actions in the 1980s. She wanted to be unheard. She wanted to be silent. She did not want her voice to attract attention. The immigrant, the migrant, the economic refugee, the asylum seeker, the epitome of the disregarded, how often do they themselves try to disappear, to meld into the background, to go unnoticed, to become invisible? As the need arises, my mother would answer. The immigrant, after all, always has to be practical. It was practical, she points out, to put a latch on the letter box after the IRA pub bombings because of retaliations. It was nothing more than that. It was an Irish house on an English street and she didn't want to come home with the shopping and find there had been anything put through there other than the post. When you belong to a suspect community, more suspect than the average immigrant, you take precautions. Even if they knew you weren't in the IRA, couldn't get a message to Gerry Adams, they might, I don't know, send a message to them via you. Better to be safe.

They, the English, the host population, could never pronounce my mother's name. There was something in that for my mother. Sure it was a little frustrating, a little further disregard. Sure it was a little bewildering. But it was also a triumph. She gave up correcting them. There is something there for the immigrant, something of value, in having a secret, unknown name. She got used, too, to automatically spelling her surname when asked for it, we all did, got used, too, to it being corrected as if she, the immigrant, had somehow got her own name wrong. She sat there and she laughed. They have no idea what I'm called and even when I tell them they don't hear.

She laughed but she admitted that, perhaps, they were right. She never did stop being an immigrant. She didn't think it from one minute to the next, didn't do anything but be human in the city, but she always was. She was always from somewhere else, had made that the case the moment she got off the boat. That, she laughed, is the immigrant's lot. I can't go around, she said, talking about home as being back there and then blame someone else for pointing it out. I can't go home in the summer, home, home, home, and expect the neighbours not to notice.

I wouldn't mind a day off every now and then but it's okay. I'm an immigrant. I won't deny it. I'm an immigrant but I still have to get the shopping in. So, I don't mind being a secret, having my own, unknown, unpronounceable name. A secret is okay.

CHRISTY CARROLL

Most immigrants do not meet Alan Kurdî's fate. Most migrants don't, most asylum seekers don't and, even, most refugees don't. That is not much to be able to say but it is something. It is something that my mother and my father safely got off the boat they got on, that the boat was seaworthy, that they arrived somewhere that whilst not, perhaps, particularly welcoming, was accepting. It doesn't mean, though, that we can say of immigrants or migrants or refugees that their fate is a comforting one or even, in fact, one we can accurately catalogue. When the so-called Calais jungle was demolished in March 2016, and the refugees there were evicted, 129 lone children disappeared.[7] Where did those kids go? Where are they now? Those children? This was a state-sanctioned, state-organised operation and still

---

[7] Kate Evans, *Threads: From the Refugee Crisis* (Verso, 2017).

129 lone children, that is children without an accompanying adult, went missing. They were unaccounted for. In an age of personal curating, of cataloguing the minutiae of your own passing life, can 129 children simply disappear? If they are migrant kids, immigrant children, refugee kids, it seems that they can. Whilst some of us are documenting our own lives in ever greater, ever more trivial detail, some of us have lives that are drifting offline completely. Drifting away. Drifting out of sight. And what of all those figures thrown around of people crossing the Mediterranean or drowning in the trying? Do we actually have anything approaching reliable numbers for them? For all of those orange-clad figures bobbing around between the dark waves? In 1957, in one year alone, one sample year from the list of Ireland's lost emigrant decades, 60,000 people left.[8] 60,000 people became immigrants, migrants, economic refugees. Over the entire decade some half a million. In

---

[8]   Keogh, O'Shea, Quinlan, *Ireland: The Lost Decade in the 1950s* (Mercier, 2004).

2017, just seventy years later, just one average life later, around 172,000 people crossed the Mediterranean into Europe.[9] The year before it had been nearer 360,000.[10] In 2017 3,118 people were thought to have drowned in the Mediterranean whilst trying to get into Europe.[11] Whilst trying to emigrate, whilst becoming migrants, whilst being refugees? The year before the drowned had amounted to 5,143.[12] The Geneva-based International Organisation for Migration called the 2017 figures 'extremely positive developments.'[13] Because only 172,000 crossed the dark sea in rickety boats, because only 3,118 drowned. That's positive. That's where we are.

But figures, like the global population of refugees amounting to the twenty-first-largest country in the world suggest one thing but say nothing.[14] Numbers don't flee coun-

9   International Organisation for Migration, 2018.
10   Ibid.
11   Ibid.
12   Ibid.
13   Ibid.
14   UNHCR, September 2016.

tries. Numbers don't drown. For instance, I could have told you there were loads of Irish in British cities, loads of us in those old industrial centres, simply by recounting my experience of growing up. I knew I wasn't having a singular experience in that English city of mine, I knew I was surrounded by Irish immigrants, Irish families having an experience much like my own. The naked statistics of just how many of us there were, well, I'm not sure how much to the story they add. They tell us something for sure, I'm not supporting a retreat from facts, not now, not when we've seen where that ends up, but the bold numbers only tell us so much. As to so much more, so much more of so much more depth, of so much more truth, they are silent. In fact, don't they camouflage some other facts, don't they camouflage the fact that this is people we are talking about? Flesh-and-blood people like the young woman standing by the railings looking back at the receding lights of home. She's not one of a decade's half a million, she's not part of some imaginary State made up of the lost and homeless. I can see her and she's not. I can see her black hair and her skin. I can reach out and hold her hand. I can hold her safe above the water. Safe above the water unlike so many others like her. If we can say that most of those don't meet Alan Kurdî's fate, we have to also say that, for a lot of the others, we don't really know what their fate is. The 172,000 or the 363,000. We can say it about migrants in general and, fittingly enough, about the children too, the other child refugees, the child migrants and child immigrants. The 129 in Calais. We can say it about the other three-year-olds. We can say that most of them don't drown. That's about it. But beyond that? Still, they don't drown. That is something. Isn't it?

The 1950s generation of Irish people washing up in English cities didn't drown. They didn't bob around in the cold Irish Sea in life jackets that didn't inflate. When they died there was a death notice in the newspaper. After a long illness bravely borne. Deeply missed by a loving family. In the loving care of these anonymous streets. Immigrant life, in a way, is at its most noticeable when it ends. When it dies. The rest of the time it is cleaning the building when everyone else has gone home. It is at the end of a corridor most people are not even aware exists. The young man coming over on the boat with the young woman, the one who will marry her in England and raise six children with her, gets any number of jobs in boom-time England. For a long time he has two, one in the day and one in the evening when he gets in from work. Gets in from work and goes back out to work again. That's how immigration works. That's how immigrants work. Sometimes at work, working night shifts, he gives in and falls asleep. He is down beneath the main city hall, the council house to top them all, minding the boilers that heat the cavernous, empty halls. The immigrant at the end of the corridor most people are not even aware exists. He sleeps even though he's not allowed to because sometimes his body will not allow him to stay awake. He closes his eyes and, in and out of hypnagogic sleep, wakes to toxic parachutes of dust floating around him. The lining from the boiler snows upon his head, upon his shoulders and his arms. A shroud of the finest asbestos cloth. He tells us this years later, tells us in passing, the asbestos immigrant. We listen, listen to the accent of the immigrant, aware of our own local voices, conscious of all the byways of immigrant life, wonder how our voices must sometimes be to him, how we sound like the people he arrived amongst. When he woke at the end of the corridor most people weren't even aware existed, did he hear his children's voices and wonder was he still asleep? A friend of his he came over with, someone from the same county, an uncle who wasn't our uncle, died years later in hospital and when his wife turned up he was hanging out of the side of the bed. They phoned her but forgot to even pull the curtains around him, the bedsheets over him. His asbestos lungs gave in and the immigrant was finally there for all to see. In death the immigrant is there for any who care to look.

It little matters at the end that they might be citizens of the twenty-first-largest State in the world. It little concerned my mother that she might have been part of a State that didn't exist, an imaginary country. She'd already left one place and was staying in another. She didn't need a third, especially one that wasn't really there. That country of refugees and migrants and immigrants isn't one we know anything about. It is the most mysterious country of all. We can't cross its borders or visit the interior. We don't know how to get there or how to get around it. We don't know if the terrain is mountaintop or lush forest. We don't know if there are lakes or forests. Most of all, we don't really know who lives there. We don't know the inhabitants or where they actually live and what they do. We can't find this country and we don't know what has happened to most of its inhabitants. We don't know, for instance, where 129 of its children are. We don't know if it really was just 3,118 of its citizens that drowned. We can't locate all of its three-year-olds. We don't know who cleans its buildings at night or even if those corridors actually exist. We don't know why we don't pull the curtains around its dead or why they lie falling from the bed. We don't even know if the citizens of that country know they are citizens of that country. We don't know if the man wearing the asbestos shroud knows or if the young woman looking back from the rails knows. She is an immigrant and we don't know what she knows at all. Whether she knows where she is or whether she is just passing through.

EAVAN BOLAND

In all the ways that matter immigrants are from an older world. The other has another place. It is a world they are always leaving, have always left, a world they broke behind them and cannot return to and it is the relationship with that world that surrounds them. It follows them and reminds them. The immigrant has managed to become a stranger in two countries. The Irish novelist John McGahern wrote of a 'whole generation of Irish people who had been forced into England to earn their bread. While there was some who prospered and did well there were others who experienced great hardship and there were many that fell by the wayside. These people, forced into England through no fault of their own, were often looked down on, most unjustly looked down upon, by some whose only good was that they managed to remain at home.'[15]

---

[15]   John McGahern, *Amongst Women* (Faber, 1990).

One of the ironies is that it is so easy to focus on the acceptance or the hostility the immigrant, the migrant, the refugee faces from the people they arrive amongst, the host community. It is so easy to look at a picture of the immigrant and only look at what is around them. To look at them as if they are just the picture. To see them existing in just that moment. We forget what's outside. We forget to look behind them. We forget, even when we insist they don't belong here, that they should and could go back, we forget that there is still a place they started out. That there is a back where they came from. We forget there are people there they have left behind. We forget that every day, the immigrant, the migrant, the refugee, is from somewhere else.

The Irish left and in doing so concentrated more than ever on being Irish. My mother was Irish in England every time she opened her mouth, every time she spoke. Her syntax and her vocabulary spoke of her whenever she said anything. Her syntax and her vocabulary spoke of where she came from. Her syntax and her vocabulary spoke of the last remaining structures of her old life. She became an accent and a set of phrases. She became Irish far more than she ever would have been if she'd stayed in Ireland. Nobody in Ireland walks around being Irish all day. That is reserved for the Irish immigrant. It is the immigrant and the migrant and the refugee who becomes their old country. The Irish in Britain, in the large, sprawling urban centres of the United Kingdom, focused in on their own Irishness as if it was the one thing they had left. They had social clubs and pubs and Irish dancing and Mass and First Holy Communion and funerals that went on for days. They insisted on their own Irishness as much as the country they'd arrived in insisted on it too. They were in agreement. It is the place left behind that was in discord.

Having left the immigrant is different. In a way the immigrant has broken some kind of national agreement, even if the state itself is broken or has forced them to leave.

The Irish who left were destined to leave. The Irish historian J.J. Lee put this quite succinctly when he noted 'there was no room at the Irish inn for those who showed their deplorable lack of breeding by being born in a labourer's cottage.'[16] Emigration wasn't a lottery or a chance occurrence. If it was a national accident it was an accident of birth and Ireland knew this. A society doesn't watch thousands of its people leaving and have no idea why it is happening or who it is happening to. In the 1950s the government was admitting that emigration was a useful 'safety valve.'[17] As recently as 1987 a senior Irish politician was insisting that we couldn't all live on a small island.[18] Presumably he also meant that some of us could. This wasn't a country wringing its hands over thousands of young people leaving. Over the young woman glancing back from the railings of the boat. Eavan

---

[16] J.J. Lee, ibid.
[17] J.J. Lee, ibid.
[18] Brian Lenihan, Snr.

Boland admitted that, instead, Irish society watched them leave on the boat, into the dark night and the black water, and 'like oil lamps we put them out/of our houses, of our minds.'[19] It was necessary for the cohesion of Irish society that emigration occur and necessary for that cohesion for it to be cloaked in silence. People emigrated into silence and around that silence was a simmering resentment.

She is asked in the summer, walking between the high hawthorn of a lane, if she is home from England. There are snags and tugs in the question. It is the kind of thing said just as easily to a tourist, a welcoming and a distance at the same time. She hears her children's voices on an Irish street and she knows others hear them too, neighbours, brothers and sisters, visitors home for the summer. She wonders when this began. When she held her baby in the ward of Heathfield Road Hospital in the inner city, where decades later summer riots would

---

[19]   Eavan Boland, *The Journey* (Carcanet, 1987).

begin, riots that spread throughout the inner-city streets of Britain, she wondered was it an Irish baby she held. She wondered did the kind nurses and cleaners look over and think there's the Irish couple with their baby, their Irish baby. Or did they see an English child. She wonders now about her own brothers and sisters, those who have stayed, who have remained at home. Do they think here she is, home from England, back from England, with her children, her children with their English accents? There is little point in pretending she left but stayed at the same time. There is no point in going over the Irish Sea and pretending there is no distance involved. Those who stayed have remained in a place she has not. They have stayed and she has raised her family else-where. It is a comment upon them as much as her. She knows that and they know that. They know what that says. About her and about them. They have to look down on her or otherwise they'd have to look down on themselves.

During the latest swarm of Irish emigration, after the economic collapse of 2008, Irish politicians, across party lines, spoke again and again about 'donning the green jersey.'[20] This clumsy sporting metaphor was a way of suggesting that, despite the financial mess we were in, it was a time for patriotic endeavours on behalf of the country. These endeavours, of course, involved taking a pay cut or forfeiting on a mortgage, or accepting the blame for a mess you didn't create, a boom time party you weren't invited to. For the thousands that emigrated it seemed donning the green jersey meant getting the hell out of the place. Yet, in doing so, they were also letting the side down. They were put on the transfer list and then looked down upon for accepting a move.

She went to England. She bailed out. The immigrant, the migrant, the refugee, has gone off into silence and said something very clearly. Those still at home have heard this and they fear what it sounds like. The

---

[20] *Journal.ie*, January 20, 2012.

immigrant, always from an older world, breeds resentment there too. The immigrant, after all that, has three places she doesn't belong to; the place she left behind, the place she's in, and the twenty-first-largest State in the world.

MICK OR PADDY

Being an immigrant was the most fun it was possible to have. It was a liberation. She left, nearly staying, nearly pulled back in, her nerve just about holding. She'd heard the dangers of being an 'emigrant girl', of leaving the confined safety of Catholic Ireland.[21] She knew there was a special betrayal in leaving and a further special betrayal in being a woman who did so. It was all part of the contortion of emigration. She had been born to a farm labourer and his wife, her mother a mother of thirteen, and when they finally settled in a corporation house they had so little that she still ended up living with her grandparents. She left school at fourteen to work in a factory making carpets, having never lived in a place that had them. Uneducated in 1950s Ireland she could have little or she could have nothing. That is what society told her.

---

[21] J.J. Lee, ibid.

That is what Ireland offered her and it was a reminder. If she ever wanted a family what did she think Ireland would offer them? Yet, still she was aware, emigration was not seen as fully respectable and certainly the children of respectable families were not expected to undergo it. There was a stigma attached to it. A stigma of defeat, of betrayal, of something lesser. It was for some but not for others. Even as it was what she was expected to do, what had been in store for her the day she was born in that cottage to those people, was one amongst the thousands whose Irish fate it was, it was something not quite right. Something that not-quite-right people did. Who wanted, after all, to say that their child was over in Birmingham or Luton? Who would want to boast of that? It was fine for the likes of her, one of thirteen raised by her grandparents, but it wasn't fine in itself. This is the immigrant's condition. To be blamed for having no choice. To be held to account for doing what you are supposed to do. To be made to feel guilty.

So in response to guilt, that ever present, gnawing guilt, that Irish thing, that Catholic thing, the immigrants responded. They responded by an insistence on having good times. That is what young people do and immigrants and migrants and refugees are usually young, full of life's hope, full of a belief in possibilities. The possibilities, even, of an evening, of one night, of a night out. I have a photograph of immigrants right here beside me now. It is a photograph of too-colourful clothes and long hair. There is a whiskey glass on the arm of a sofa. Somebody is sitting in somebody's lap. The uncle who will die on display in a hospital bed is smiling at the camera, his eyes drink-glassy, even from this distance. They are in their early forties by this stage, the immigrants, the young woman from the railings on the boat. She is perhaps twenty-five years away by now, twenty-five years or so an immigrant. There she is, off to one side, smiling, still standing, dancing. I remember them more years later, well into their fifties by now, on Sunday afternoons in an immigrant Irish social club called, without irony, The Emerald. This was to see them released, see the immigrants escaped from their long, overtime week, out from the building everyone else has left, away from the corridor no one else knows is there. It was to see an abandon engendered by immigrant life. By all of the coarseness of hard, physical work, of undisguised bottom-end jobs, of the complex strands of living elsewhere. This is drinking and dancing as response. There is a song about every county and drinks spill on carried trays. There are mothers and fathers here and daughters and sons. These are esoteric afternoons and the city outside is unaware, utterly unaware, that this part of England exists. Any English person I ever brought here was another tourist in their own country. There are no traditional costumes but here, live, is the hidden immigrant life. It is hours and hours of calibrated carelessness. Monday will still come and children will still go to school and people will still get up for work but for now there is something akin to joy. It is sticky tables and queues at the bar. For now the immigrants, always full of being immigrants, always Irish, shake off their tiredness, their weariness, shake off their frustration at having to be Irish and insist on it. Immigrants are by definition defined by someone else, by a bureaucratic system or a passing stranger. They have names the host population cannot pronounce or chooses not to hear, hearing only Mick or Paddy instead. They have accents they cannot escape and surnames that mark them out. They are accountable for events and political occurrences they know nothing about. They are tied to the place they came from even though it is just the place they come from, not the place they exist in, live in and love in. They are bound by the status others give them as if they never quite got off the boat. They have to think on their feet because they have to think constantly about being what they are categorised as being. They just want to go to work, talk to the children, fall asleep, walk along the street like it was their street. Escape the vague sense of continuous dislocation. Leave behind, for just a moment, that nagging feeling of not quite belonging. So they take the afternoon and turn it on its head and for a few moments embrace this forced Irishness and make it their own. They celebrate being immigrants in a way that, well, only immigrants can. They decide that being an immigrant is the most fun it is possible to have.

At the conclusion of these afternoons and at the conclusion of any similar nights something specific takes place. The afternoons do not, of course, end in a regular fashion, they end in dribs and drabs, not full stops. There is a last drink and, then, a last drink. Someone starts a song, another conversation, a fight. Someone comes back in looking for somebody else. Definitive arrangements are made to meet again in a few hours, to carry on, to continue, to not go home and fall asleep, to not wake three hours from now and renege.

The arrangements are made every week, Sunday after Sunday, and the Irish spill out onto the English streets and the other immigrants walk by. But the clear delineation in the afternoon or the night is always the same. There are a couple of recognisable drumbeats and chairs are pushed back and the conversation ceases. The whole room, the men, the women, the children, are standing and some are singing and they are singing in Irish the national anthem of the country they left. The young woman who leant against the railings of the boat and looked back at the receding lights of the harbour is standing too. And there they all are, in a room on an English street, the immigrants standing in salute to a country they all left, that couldn't contain them. They stand until the music ends and they stand in defiance. They stand and they are standing still and they are immigrants and they are a contradiction.

JEREMY CLARKSON

Of course, there is something about the immigrant, the migrant, the refugee that attracts notions. There are shades to this, both dark and light. The light, which we shall come to later, isn't as benign as it thinks it is, but is naïve and condescending more than hostile. The dark is the straightforward othering of people, the distancing of them from ordinary considerations. It might be seen in the crude minds of the tabloid press, might usefully be apportioned just to them, most obviously to them. But that wouldn't be true. Such notions, such crude, reduced and reductive ways of thinking are held just as much in refined circles too. It has served, for instance, a certain narrative to explain Brexit by reference to an inarticulate white working-class rage, as if only those people possessed minds that reflected back those of *The Sun*, *The Star*, *The Daily Mail*. It's not true though, is it? The establishment, the elite, has long voiced its own notions about immigrants and migrants and refugees and it has not done so in a sophisticated way. What is most striking, for the overhearing immigrant, the listening migrant, the ears-cocked refugee, the young woman leaning against the boat railings, is the casual, confident tone.

Squeezed in between Enoch Powell's 'rivers of blood' speech and Norman Tebbit's cricket test of loyalty, Margaret Thatcher introduced the notion of being 'swamped' by immigrants. Margaret Thatcher, graduate of Oxford University, fretting about 'people of a different culture'.[22] Some years later Defence Secretary Michael Fallon echoed his erstwhile leader's words when he too talked about being 'swamped' and painted a picture of a Britain 'under siege from large numbers of migrant workers and people claiming benefits'.[23] Michael Fallon, an alumnus of Epsom College. David Cameron, of Eton

---

[22]   TV interview, *World in Action*, January 27th, 1978.
[23]   *The Guardian*, October 27th, 2014.

College, poetically reimagined the notion by talking about refugees as a 'swarm' instead of a swamp and by talking about those in Calais as a 'bunch of migrants'. In one speech he went even further by exclaiming that they 'are economic migrants and they want to enter Britain illegally and the British people and I want to make sure our borders are secure and you can't break into Britain without permission'.[24] In David Cameron's words it seemed as if economic migrants, like those standing straight-backed for the national anthem of another state, those failing the cricket test, were burglars. His school chum, Boris Johnson, attracted more by the loose-tongued, comedy racism of Prince Philip, talked of people in the Commonwealth as being 'flag waving picaninnies' and on a visit to Myanmar recited a poem by the author of 'The White Man's Burden'.[25] Theresa May proudly authored vans to drive around England bearing a slogan telling immigrants

---

[24]   *The Guardian*, January 27th, 2016.
[25]   *The Telegraph*, January 10th, 2002.

to 'go home.'[26] Theresa May, of St. Hugh's College, the University of Oxford, using the language of the BNP to write on the side of a white van. Nigel Farage, once of Dulwich College, spoke of British people having their 'noses rubbed in diversity' and stood in front of a Breaking Point poster that depicted a snaking line of brown-faced refugees.[27] This was just a few days after the MP Jo Cox was murdered by a man shouting 'Britain First'. It all, somehow, makes a comment about traditional costumes seem just an embarrassing social gaffe.

Immigrants hear all of this. Refugees and migrants hear it too. How could they not? It is spoken about them. It is spoken to them. It's not as if they sit deliberately tuned to the mutterings of establishment MPs or, and this is not as random as it sounds, well-paid motoring journalists. But it is spoken to them and once spoken in one place it goes on to enter the wider discourse. Once there,

---

[26]   *The Independent*, April 19th, 2018.
[27]   *The Guardian*, June 16th, 2016.

it is up for grabs. It begins by being spoken at them, the immigrants, the migrants, the refugees, and ends being, perhaps, shouted at them from a passing vehicle. And how startling it is to hear just how much the very comfortable despise those with the very least. How much, for instance, Nigel Farage or David Cameron both feared and loathed those who were, literally, living in tents. Who had no possessions and, in some cases, no actual State left behind them. No country to return to, to go home to. Remember too that this casual disregard is heard in a context not in a vacuum. And how strange it is to contrast this easy disregard for others, the immigrants, the migrants, the refugees, with the value put on others. If, for instance, Jeremy Clarkson, an alumnus of Repton School, can punch an Irishman for not having his dinner ready and people respond on Facebook with 'je suis Clarkson',[28] could it be said this is because some people are disregarded and, in Clarkson's

---

[28] *Marketwatch.com*, March 11th, 2015.

case, some people are extra-regarded? Is it because in some minds some people are still cleaning, even when they are not, the building where everyone else has gone home, are still working at the end of a corridor Jeremy Clarkson doesn't even know exists? Jeremy Clarkson, the well-paid motoring journalist, another old pal of David Cameron's, once broadcast a joke sketch about the best way of smuggling a migrant in a car. Immigrants hear this. Refugees and migrants hear it too.

Growing up in an Irish family in Britain was not to face fear of deportation. It was not even to visually stand out. We could look and sound just like the host population. It was not to feel an overt alienation. It was to feel part of the city we were in, part of the inner-city core of it, part of urban England at its most urban, English self. And yet. And yet there was always this slight feeling. Immigrant families, immigrant communities, feel a remove. It might, in a white Irish case, especially that of their children, the children of the men and women on the boat, be slight in comparison to others. To other others. But it is still there. This feeling of not being English or British, not properly anyway. Not fully paid-up members. Not fully part of the whole. When it comes to emphasis, when it comes to things like street parties for the Jubilee of 1977, for Royal Weddings say, or a football World Cup, the emphasis of nation. That is when there is a remove. That is when you have to mind the gap. Sunday afternoons standing to the national anthem of one country does not easily translate to waving the bunting of another. Immigrants feel other. They feel it all the time, feel it often, feel it only sometimes. Feel it only on occasions. And on the occasions they don't, there is usually a voice reminding them that they should.

ROBERT ELMS

The writer and photographer Robert Elms wrote a book back in 1988 called *In Search of the Craic*. This is no crude example of othering but is, instead, an urbane sophisticate's search for the authentic experience of living like an Irishman in London. The 'craic' is represented as something almost mystical that the Irish have direct access to but that others can only see the outline of. Elms, a suburban southerner, can trace the presence of the craic but he doesn't have the aboriginal soul that would allow him to truly live it. That is the preserve of those from that distant, mist-covered island to the west. It is the inheritance of the craic-blessed Irish. In its treatment of the Irish the book is nothing if not affectionate, which was welcome enough in the grim IRA-bracketed 1980s. It is also representative of that condescending treatment so often dished out to immigrants, migrants and refugees. In this version it is so utterly charming to see people engaged in their traditional pastimes of, not going to work or paying the bills or minding the kids, but hanging around the portals to the entrance of that mysterious land of craic. In this light, benign treatment of the immigrant, the other, they are not diminished by dehumanising speech, they are categorised by their nearness to a rawness, an original state, that the host population has lost.

In this way immigrants are more authentic, more natural. They are wilder, more like children or animals. In this way they might live on society's edge not because of deprivation or inequality but because that is more their natural habitat. They are more the strangeness that is them than they ever will be the regular that is us. The young woman on the boat, looking back from the railings, will endure not because she has to but because she has something of the rainbow-arched fields and the black rivers about her. The savagery her countrymen will inflict years later on the urban city she lives in, by putting bombs in ordinary pubs, is explicable because they have something of savagery within them. The heartbreak it causes her is explicable because she has something of the twilight soul within her. Humans doing terrible, human things and other humans responding with shattered human sadness doesn't apply here. It doesn't explain. These are immigrants.

My uncle, the young woman's brother, lived three streets away from us in the inner city. One day in the bleak early fog of the 1980s I went with him to the back of a row of houses earmarked for demolition. We were pulling up floorboards to use in making a shed. We were tatting. At one stage the door of an outside shed came open and a kid sniffing glue, the bag around his nose and mouth, fell out. *In Search of the Craic*, and a hundred other representations like it, would have you believe that because we were Irish this came naturally to us, the scavenging, the licentiousness of having fuck all. Would it not be more truthful, more intellectually honest, to say that this was a simple, unexaggerated, picture of '80s urban decay? Of the real state of British inner cities, inner cities that would erupt in street rioting within a few short years? Did our Irishness, in that context, only exist in the eye of the beholder?

The example, of course, of some aspect of even the most benign stereotype is the truth of its falsehood. The truth of the Emerald Club on a Sunday afternoon. Even well in to the 1990s I could have shown to anyone pubs full of single, suited, v-necked-jumper-wearing Irishmen who had barely altered from the day they got off the boat. These men never integrated. They never thought of integrating. They lived a solitary, west-of-Ireland, rural bachelor lifestyle, on the long, brick streets of England. My uncle, the young woman's brother, was one of those men. His accent never changed. He never swapped the sing-song, up-and-down hills of Cork in his voice for the flat vowels of industrial England. He worked with other

Irishmen, drank with other Irishmen. Had the craic with other Irishmen. I have on my wall here where I write this a cut-out cover to an old LP called *Paddy in the Smoke*, subtitled *Irish Dance Music from a London Pub*. The cover is two men in suits and trilby hats dancing on the street outside a pub. They are stylish and recognisably Irish. They look a little wild. They look a little other. They look released, as if no confinement of the city can contain them. They seem, almost, to be dancing to a music only they can hear. They look as if they are having the craic. I recall one St. Patrick's Day in the city we grew up in, a city whose St. Patrick's Day parade was cancelled for over twenty years because of IRA bombings. On the day it returned, in 1996, we got a lift back in the early evening in the back of a friend's truck. We were happy, full of cheer and drink, a bit giddy. My mother, my father and a few others were in the truck. The truck was an open-air flatbed and as it drove up the main street of the inner city area we lived in I was standing up at the front looking out. I was standing up in the open back of the truck. I imagine we must have looked a little wild, a little other. But, you know, it was St. Patrick's Day. We were having the craic. Immigrants, after all, play up sometimes to the notion of being immigrants, insist upon it. Being other is a powerful riposte, especially for the powerless, for those who do not even know the usual corridors of power exist. Being other is a handy escape. Being other, when you know you're being observed as just that, when you know other is expected of you, well, it can be hard to resist. When you know you're seen as having the keys to the enchanted, mist-laden land of the craic, it is hard not to pretend you have those very keys in your hand.

She has to get up on Monday, though, just like everybody else. She doesn't hum a rain-tinged refrain walking down the street. She doesn't look out of the bus window and see the whole of the moon when you only see the crescent. She doesn't have a line of poetry to help you through a tough day.

She's still a little homesick, for sure, the boat and the cold metal rail, still an immigrant, a migrant, a refugee. But she's mainly just a woman.

THE ROYAL FAMILY

She will remember her son standing up in the truck because her son standing up in the truck is an anomaly. That is not what they did. Being so wilfully visible is not an immigrant trait.

Immigrants, migrants, refugees, are not, by and large, urban people. They become so but they do not often begin so. It is the city that draws them, that pulls them. The city creates them. They come in from the damp fields and the arid mountains and the barren soil. Some for sure have fled cities that have imploded, are fleeing gunshots from behind a street corner, the smell of death and rubble, but even they are not used to these places, these cities that only exist as cities, that have no palimpsest. On arriving in the city, on getting off the boat, the young woman felt consumed. It wasn't just the buildings, the hey, mum, I think that chimney is onto you, it was the entire sensory experience of an industrial city. Cork was a city, for sure, but there are cities and there are cities. It is a matter of scale and for the young woman on the boat the dislocation of emigration was married to the overwhelming insistence of the city itself. She felt the city as a physical pressure, looming over her, weighing her down. The brick intensity of it. The colour and the noise. The sheer number of people. The mathematical distance between where she'd left and where she'd arrived could not have been more obvious. A city built around transport, a city moving within and across itself, a city always going somewhere else. She responded the only way she could. She hung on but she withdrew. She hadn't come this far, the immigrant, the migrant, the refugee cannot afford to fold, just to turn back again. She continued but she stepped to one side. The city did not defeat her but it did smother her. It became a way of moving, a way of behaving. Immigrants, migrants, refugees, often so noticeable, often so strikingly visible, become adept at disappearing. They learn the value of anonymity, the worth of the crowd, the city itself. The city becomes their camouflage. Vulnerability comes from standing out. It comes from being noticed. She learns quickly, her head down, intimidated month after month by the physicality of her surroundings, about moving through the city unnoticed. She realises that if she keeps her mouth shut, if she can avoid being heard, and oh how loud the city is, how much noise it contains, creates, the city will ignore her. Her status is always there, always lurking in the background, her immigration. She knows it even when she thinks she doesn't. The city, though, is careless and the city couldn't care less. If she moves through it unseen, unnoticed, the city expresses no interest in her at all. The idea that immigrants should bring attention to themselves is anathema to her. The idea that they might parade themselves in an open-air truck. She does not deny her Irishness, her immigration, but she is happier, more at ease, when it is left unremarked. When she walks home, with the shopping bags, in silence.

When a nation adorns itself, flags itself for all to see, there are those within it who become unbearably self-conscious. Those times when a nation declares it wants to be noticed. The 1977 street parties for the Royal Jubilee were held across Britain. The inner-city street, outside her front door, house after house along the tight terraces, was lined with trestle tables. Everyone was invited and nobody was uninvited. She recalls it with a shiver of discomfort. From one side of the street to the other they raised Union Jack bunting. The red, white and blue fluttering in the sunlight and the running, screaming children. It is not that she even has any strong feelings about the Royal Family. She is not particularly Republican when it comes to this. She could, in fact, be labelled a Royal Family sympathiser, following them in a slightly soap-opera kind of way. She finds it, if she ever thinks about it, a peculiarly British obsession but, then, this a peculiarly British country. She has been invited, no one on the street has not, and, of course, she accepts. She has to accept. She knows full well that not accepting would only draw attention. Not accepting would make them stand out and they already stand out. She is already introduced with the words, this is my neighbour, she's Irish and she's got six kids. She has realised that they will stand out far more today if they stay indoors. They will have to come out, take a place at the table, eat and drink. And the vista is an English street in 1977 adorned with Union Jacks and a long, seated table of neighbours, neighbours the length of the entire street, more neighbours than the street could possibly house. She is convinced, later, that this is not deliberate, is more a matter of timing but they end up at the end of the table at the end of the street. They end up on the edge of proceedings. She is utterly convinced this is not deliberate. She is convinced it is just happenstance. They are positioned, her husband, her six children, at the tail end of this most English, most British, she's never sure which, of days. She confesses afterwards that she could not recall ever feeling so out of place. Not even in those first few months of heartsore confusion. There they sit, the Irish family, the so-many-children family, in a street scene of colourful communalism, at the end, apart, ever so slightly, oh so noticeably apart. She can't wait for it to be over, for the children to get fidgety, get bored, the vaguely uneasy but generally unaware children. She wants to go back behind the door and let them to it. She wants to get her own back inside the house, the house where the Irish family live, and close the door. She has never felt, never been made to feel, just, oh, so different. But she is convinced, she insists, it is just circumstance, just timing.

It is hard to quantify later the workings of this. Are they apart here, are they other, because the neighbours judge them to be? Are they other because they have made themselves so? Has their own dragging reluctance positioned them where they are?

Is it only a matter of timing? Or is this difference, this apartness, this othering simply an intrinsic part of their being immigrants? Is it part of their condition? Even invited to the party will they sit there looking, feeling, out of place? Are they only, the Union Jacks swaying in the breeze, waiting to return to their imaginary anonymity?

DAMIEN HIRST

Homesickness is a real thing. We tend to forget this. We tend to bracket it with puppy love or fainting at a boy-band gig. Something heightened and concentrated but not fully genuine. It is intense and ferocious, we think, but not really worthy of a fully functioning adult. It is a type of immaturity. Homesickness is writing an overwrought love letter to your imaginary self, who is at home in your bedroom, as the rain of somewhere else falls around the actual you. It is hard not to wonder if this view of homesickness doesn't stem from the British public-school system and a cadre of boarding boys learning to distrust emotion. It is unlikely that David, Boris, or Nigel would ever entertain homesickness. You can't fly around the world or sit in the European Parliament if you're yearning for your own back garden. You can't excel at anything, can't flourish in the cold chambers of commerce, if you want your mummy and daddy. You can't be manly if you suffer from a sickness of feeling. Homesickness is akin to nostalgia or sentimentality. It is a mawkish dishonesty. Homesickness is the Christmas card where a robin looks in the festive window. It is a Eurovision Song Contest of an emotion, all surface feeling. It is an artwork by Damien Hirst and we suspect that the glistening tears don't mean anything. But homesickness is a real thing even if we tend to forget this.

She describes the homesickness she felt in those early days, those early months, going on into years, as gut wrenching. She doesn't talk about dislocation or cultural alienation. I was homesick, she says, and it gave me physical pain, a pain in my heart. She thought of her grandfather and her grandmother that she grew up with. She thought of her mother and father, her brothers and sisters. She thought of what they might be doing at certain times of the day. She thought of the light or the rain or a bird calling. She thought of the voices she'd hear, the accents. She thought of the silence at night. She thought of all of this with her head on the pillow in the dark and a tightness in her chest. She thought of it because she could not help but do so. She was newly married, soon to be pregnant. She was not indulging herself. She was merely a young woman in a country that wasn't her own. She was merely a young woman, she thought, in the wrong country. It was not a luxury to feel this. It was debilitating. It was a sadness. She had barely been out of her home county and now she was in a different country with different people and different words and a different way of behaving. She wasn't visiting, she wasn't an interested or distant tourist. This was where she was living. This was her life. Homesickness hurt her. It wasn't immature or overwrought or ultimately dishonest. It just was.

She had felt an emotional breaking. She hadn't been sent away from home because this was her path, how her social structure was constructed. She wasn't boarding here on the strange, tight, noisy, distant streets of England. This wasn't how her parents were preparing her for adulthood, by sending her away, by creating an emotional distance. She didn't come from enough wealth and comfort to indulge in character building exercises. She was in England because she had no choice. Immigrants, migrants and refugees have no choice. They have not opted from a pile of glossy, fluffy, brochures. Having a stultified, stunted, poverty-haunted life could never be described as a choice. Yet, in another way she was very akin to David, Boris and Nigel. She had followed a preordained path. She was only ever reared for this. For leaving. For emigration. For becoming an immigrant. Like the highest echelon, where names are down for schools not long after a child is born, where David, Boris or Nigel might even get Father's old dorm, the opposite end of the pile have names down too. They are getting on the boat whilst they are a babe in arms and no one says it and everyone knows it. The very wealthy break up their own families by sending their children to boarding school. The very poorest have theirs taken off them or put in a borstal. The top and the bottom are both raised in institutions. Likewise the immigrants, the migrants, the refugees. They are doing, or having done to them, exactly what they are supposed to do.

Not that there isn't a danger of nostalgia and clogging sentimentality. There is. Maudlin is along the same bus route as homesickness. Those Sunday afternoons in The Emerald were characterised by a song for every Irish county. Everybody had to get their wistful share. 'Limerick You're a Lady'. 'Take Me Back to Mayo'. It was a time for indulging homesickness. Like picking a sore tooth. No long-term damage done but a safe reminder that it is there. This isn't the pain in the heart. It is a toying with sadness, sadness as a concept, as a song, as a sweetness. There is a darker side too and it is not just the black rivers of drink, the illusory oblivion of alcohol. An Irish band called The Wolfe Tones, named after a defeated Irish patriot, sang songs that spoke of the emigrant experience. Songs like, 'My Heart is in Ireland', with lyrics like 'with the Birmingham Irish I sang songs of home.' Their stock in trade though, their overwhelming repertoire, was a volley of nationalist songs about armed conflict. These songs glorified Irish Nationalism and revelled in the conflict between Britain and Ireland. If the Provisional IRA had a house band it was The Wolfe Tones. It wasn't even that most of those listening shared their views or that the Irish in Britain were all convinced supporters of the IRA. Far from it. It was more that the very real homesickness of thousands of people, the very existent psychology and emotion, meant that they were vulnerable to crude reductions of the idea of home. It is one thing to sing idealised lyrics about your home place but quite another to embrace simplified histories about bloodshed. Homesickness is indeed a real thing but some of the ideas of home it embraces are very much not.

She would say it even now, decades and decades on. I was sick, I was sad, I was wrong inside. I'd left home and that is a harsh place to be. I didn't want to be homesick, I wasn't wallowing, though maybe, the odd Sunday afternoon, much later, I did. I was an immigrant and I was homesick and I know it was real. I know it was real because I was there.

VERLYN KLINKENBORG

There is a book called *The Last Fine Time* by Verlyn Klinkenborg. It is set in Buffalo, New York, and is an imaginative recounting of everyday life in that city. It is also about the Polish-speaking immigrants that lived there in big numbers. It is a beautiful, evocative book. It is, in true reflection of the immigrant life, about two places, Buffalo and old Europe. The place arrived in and the place left. In one chapter Klinkenborg recounts in detail the walls of a particular immigrant's house. He describes a picture of the old Austrian Emperor and his family that adorns one of the sitting room walls. 'This old-fashioned gravure hangs on the upstairs, back-apartment, dining-room wall of 722 Sycamore Street. It is a more striking icon than the ceramic Sacred Heart hanging across the room or the statue of the Virgin Mary in the opposite corner. The Sacred Heart, whether or not the image itself is reverenced, burns for all Buffalonians; religion overlies their buzzing and humming like an anointed shroud. But the Emperor of Austria-Hungary surrounded by his heirs, this family gathering from the pages of the *Almanach de Gotha,* that yearbook of kings! It is an icon that suffuses the brisk American air with languor. It perfumes the room with deference. Looked at long enough, it would produce a stoop in the shoulders of many émigrés. But to Thomas Wenzek it is a last faint homage to Emperor Franz Josef I and to Austria-Hungary.'[29] The immigrant's house is an immigrant's house. It has things only an immigrant's house would have. Things that denote the fact an immigrant lives here. The interior immigrant life is apart, it is at a remove. It is at a remove both mentally and physically.

The young woman at the railing of the boat has a house, years later, where she lives with her husband and her six children. It

---

[29]   Verlyn Klinkenborg, *The Last Fine Time* (Alfred A Knopf, 1991).

is a council house with two bedrooms and through the door of one bedroom a small box room used as another bedroom. It is in a line of long streets of terraced housing, of chimneys and blue slate roofs. It is the industrial city as it grew, as it built itself. It is the inner city, the inner ring of the city itself and in the older houses, on the wider streets, doctors and lawyers once lived. Within living memory, as an older, English neighbour tells her, the street above there, Charles Road, was full of maids busily crossing, professional men coming home from the city in the evening. The area was known for the fine quality of its air and there was a nearby sanatorium for TB sufferers. By the time the young woman gets off the boat that is all long gone. A few older English residents remain, with memories of the war and bomb shelters in their gardens, but the wealthy have moved further out from the city again. These streets are now populated by immigrants and the area is now a poorer one and the inner city as a social and political problem is growing. For the young woman, though, it is a welcome place to rear her children. It is a much-loved place. It is a house full of young children running, playing and arguing. The Irish couple are content there. They might even be at home there but home is a loaded word for immigrants, migrants, refugees. Home isn't bandied about carelessly.

What it clearly is, though, is an Irish house. An Irish house on an English street. Not just an Irish house, an immigrant house, because those around it know it as such. Not just an Irish house, an immigrant house, because the host population know it to be so. An Irish house. The front door opens straight onto the street. Step through it and this front room, the best room, has a clock that is in the shape of a map of Ireland. The front room, in that old tradition, is only used on occasions. When Christmas comes they move in there, to the children's excitement. Space is at a premium in a two-bedroomed house with six kids but the tradition of the best furniture and the unused chairs is kept. The clock is gaudy. Bright, shiny green. But it depicts the place left. It says something, especially here, in a house on an Irish street

The immigrant house is a paradigm of immigration. Through the best front room is the living room. It has a window onto the yard and another door through to the galley kitchen. On the small wall above and around the gas fireplace there are three religious pictures. The centrepiece is that of the Sacred Heart and the Saviour's eyes seem to follow you around the room. Wherever you sit or stand He is always looking. He is omnipresent in the small room, in the small Irish house, on the long English street. It is an English street but the adornments on the walls are those of an Irish Catholic home. At the base of the picture a cross glows red and never goes out. It never turns off. It never sleeps. It is always there and for those living there it is present but unnoticed. It is only in the years when her children are older and return with English friends from English homes that she hears her house is remarked upon, that comment is passed on the religious symbols and the Irishness of the place. It is only by the comments of others, she realises, that her own children are introduced to the particulars of their own surroundings and their own upbringing. The immigrant, the migrant, the refugee, so often a symbol, so often an image for a virulent, tabloid worldview is unconsciously besotted with her own symbols. The everyday ephemera of an immigrant life are different from those of the hosts. Different pictures, different images, different ornaments, different food and drink, different music and song. The inconsequential becomes significant. Sometimes even the immigrant doesn't know quite how much of an immigrant they are.

The Last Fine Time illustrates a universal experience through a singular account. That is the core of being a migrant. Immigration is not an abstract. It is not a study with readily defined stages. It can't be illustrated with graphs. Immigration, migration, becoming a refugee, are things that happen to people.

They are momentous only in the way that a human life is. Sometimes they are best explained by recounting the collapse of the Austro-Hungarian Empire or by examining a conflict or the vagaries of an economy. But they are also explained by cheap trinkets and a few pictures on the wall. Any immigrant could tell you that.

DONALD TRUMP

A lan Kurdî didn't get very far. He didn't get far as a refugee. He didn't get far as a migrant. He didn't get as far as a place of safety. He didn't get as far as becoming an immigrant. He didn't get very far into his life. If his death, the sodden photograph of his death, is not a modern tragedy then the modern has utterly lost its way.

The young woman on the boat went on to have six children. A family of such size was not unusual amongst Irish Catholics, however much the host population, the English neighbours, might have commented upon it. The young mother would not have stood out amongst her immigrant peers. She would not have been anything remarkable. They didn't come all of that way not to build a life and for most of them that meant building a family. For the immigrant, family becomes a lodestone, something to do with having made such a move, such a decision, in the first place. We all know the clichés about this. We know all the tales of immigrants who work as many jobs, as many hours as they can, to educate children to as high a level as they can. It is even part of the Donald Trump story. The Scottish mother and the German immigrant grandparents. Even the scourge of migrants has an immigrant background. We all know the Americanisation of the immigrant story, the way we know the Americanisation of everything else. Like most clichés, though, there is some truth in this. The young woman does spend time trying to get children into the best State Catholic schools. There is some truth in the immigrant hunger for bettering their children. Like most clichés, though, the partial truth only serves to hide the more complex, more nuanced, reality. The immigrant comes all that way and to make a simple sense of it all has a family but finds family simply becomes another strand in the complexity of immigration.

What the immigrant doesn't envisage, doesn't foresee, is that the children in this family will soon be bilingual, will soon live both in and out of the family, in a way the initial immigrant never quite manages. The Irish are, perhaps, a more startling example of this than others. They are, usually, white, usually dress akin to their hosts, usually have some, at least, shared cultural references. Most strikingly of all they have the same language. The Irish are far nearer to the English than the other immigrants. They are far less obvious than everyone else on the inner-city streets, in the immigrant-rich neighbourhoods. They can meld easier. Their children do not speak another language at home. The young woman gets off the boat and she could pass for English as she walks down the street. She bears no visual difference, or at least, none visible to anyone who isn't Irish themselves. As long as she doesn't speak, as long as her instantly defining accent is unheard, she is indistinguishable from the host nation. Of course, her English neighbours forget this, identifying her every time they see her, but they forget. They forget that if they didn't know her they couldn't pick her out from the crowd, from the city, from themselves. Of her children, she quickly realises, there is a further truth. They do not have the accent of her coastal city, of the hills and lanes. They have the architecture of factories and canals in their voices. They sound like the city. The immigrant has come all of this way and her children sound like strangers.

She swears, though, that before school, before the city became family life just as much as the house, that they sounded like their parents. She says that in the hospital in the English city the Irish couple had an Irish baby in their arms and that for years at home the child of the Irish couple sounded Irish. The child began, she says, by sounding Irish. The sound of the city drowned that out and she knows that, she hears that, but the Irishwoman realises too that her English-speaking, English-sounding children, so much now a part of the city, are not only what they sound like. The immigrant mother realises that these children too, these children of immigrants, who come from an English-speaking home and only ever speak English might only have one language. But they are still bilingual.

They are bilingual in terms of ideas and notions, if not vocabulary. To fail to acknowledge that is to fail to acknowledge the interior reality of immigrant or migrant life. It is to reduce immigrant, migrant or refugee life to a one-dimensional copy of life as led by others. It is to continue to make the immigrant both glaringly conspicuous and invisible. It is to remove complexity from the immigrant condition and if the immigrant knows anything it is complexity. Instead the young woman and her children, children with Irish names and Irish faces and English accents, acknowledge their own bilingual complications everyday. The fact that they only speak English serves to illustrate just how much the dual-language status of most other immigrants, migrants and refugees is a domestic truth of real social import.

So the children of the young woman, looking wistfully back from the railings of the boat, have that other country, the one left, inside their heads. It is on the wall of the house they grow up in and in the voices of their parents and the parents of their friends. When summer comes they are shipped back across the sea, the returning English cousins, and introduced to the hybrid condition they inhabit. You are Irish, their parents tell them. You are English, their Irish cousins tell them. You are from that Irish family, their neighbours tell them. You are English, Irish strangers tell them. You are of this city, their voices tell them. They have references and notions and assumptions that are Irish. A cultural baggage they heft with them wherever they go. They have a daily life shaped by the city and country their parents came to. They meld easily, even easier than their accent-haunted parents. They come from an immigrant house though. Their parents when they speak of coming back from work, the shops, the Emerald Club, say they are going home. Their parents when they speak of going back over the Irish Sea speak of going home, tell the children they are going home. They grow up with this, the children of the Irish woman. They grow up, whatever their accents might sound like, whatever about only having one language, as the children of immigrants, and they are bilingual.

NORMAN TEBBIT

The cricket test is as crude a measure of belonging as it is hard to imagine. 'Who do you support?' is a playground definition of identity. It is another way in which the immigrant, the migrant, the refugee is reduced and becomes the inhabitant of a merely symbolic world. There is, though, only one person more obsessed with this than Norman or Nigel or *The Daily Mail* and that is the immigrant, or the migrant, or the refugee herself. Once she puts a foot on that boat she slips into a world where identity matters. On the one hand she is beset with anxieties around becoming a deracinated chimera and on the other with the idea that she will never leave her place of origin however long she has actually left it. She fears she will become nothing but a faceless consumer living out her invisible life in the city, or she fears she will never be allowed to take off her Kiss Me I'm Irish hat, and will live out her days in the horrors of an endless St. Patrick's Day parade. The immigrant becomes an eternal adolescent, never quite sure of who she is.

The question of immigrant identity isn't just bureaucratic form-filling. It isn't a matter of the census and the peculiarly limited boxes it seeks to put us all in. The young woman gets off the boat and with no fixed vision of the future, with all of the flexible notions of youth, has no idea that she will spend the next forty years in this second country. Of course, unlike other immigrants in the days before cheaper air travel, her original country is just back over the Irish Sea. She goes back often. She manages to get back for most significant events, she is there for funerals and she brings her children 'home' each summer. But this is not a luxurious life, it is not a life of holidays and short breaks. This is an immigrant life lived on immigrant streets and in immigrant jobs. She can get to her country but she doesn't live in it.

Each night she checks on the children and puts out the light in a house on an English street. On the nights her husband is there they talk for a little while and on the nights he is working, and they are most nights because an immigrant's wage is an overtime wage, she watches the streetlight shine in past the curtains. She knows as she drifts off to sleep that her brothers and sisters and her mother are sleeping back in Ireland and they are doing this night after night. She knows that they still do mundane things each mundane day but that they do it in Ireland. She knows, because an immigrant always knows, that she is living her life in a different country from the one she began in and this means she worries about who she is. She knows she is still Irish but she knows too she is here now. The streetlight shines in through the night and she worries what this all means. She worries she will somehow drift away from her own Irishness and she worries too that she never will.

She makes a startling admission to one of her own children one time and it is a startling admission to herself too. I like to go home in the summer, she says, I need to, but I think I prefer it here in the winter. She's taken aback by this. She surprises herself. If she'd thought about it longer she might not have admitted it. It doesn't matter that it's true, she'd rather not have said it. She is unsettled by it. The immigrant and the migrant and the refugee is desperate to get to the new country, is in some cases seeing it as the only place of survival, but does not really see beyond that. The new country is the future and that is enough, the future does not have to extend too much, does not need to be measured. For the immigrant it is the leaving and the arrival that is important, everything beyond that is vague and ill-defined, imaginary. As long as the new country is still the future then the vanished home is still within reach. Immigration is a thing postponed even when it is carried out. It is a thing of stasis. The danger otherwise is that there will be admission works better here that this new place is so concrete, is so real, is so actual, that in some regards it might even be better.

She feels that the only way she can ever belong, and she feels this more as the years go on, the longer she is here in the city, is by sloughing off her Irishness. She knows she can never become English and knows she will never want to. She feels though, as the decades slip by, as she is the immigrant now for decade after decade, that she might fall into some new category, some new hybrid resident of these inner-city streets. She fears, as much as she knows she will never be English, that she will stop being Irish too. In response she worries about how much she has to assert her Irishness in order to maintain it. Must she really parade her Irishness on a regular basis to ensure it survives? How can she combine that with a consistent, regular existence? She knows that to live in England and spend so much time asserting her identity as being from somewhere else is a recipe for exhaustion. And she has six kids, she's exhausted enough.

The streetlight shines in and as each night passes she doesn't know if she is becoming more Irish or less. She does not know how much of this old, industrial city she is becoming. What, she sometimes wonders, do they think of her back in Ireland? Do they think of her now as in some part English? Do they consider the simple passage of time to have in some way claimed her, to have taken her away? If her children are bilingual what is she, this immigrant woman? Could she really claim to be as Irish as the day she left, the day she got on the boat? Immigrants, migrants and refugees are not settled people. By definition they cannot be. She's not as Irish as she was and she's not as Irish as she would have been if she'd stayed. How could she be? She is differently Irish. She is from the new place now too. She is an immigrant and it's always a test. The only way to avoid that would be to go back home. To return.

BRIAN WHELAN

The London-Irish artist and writer, Brian Whelan, has worked extensively around an idea he calls The Myth of Return. He has painted it and tussled with it in words. 'I'm not an immigrant. I was born in England and live here. But many of the concerns and ideas of my parent's generation were visited upon the second generation, my generation. For example, the 'myth of return' which I lived with all my childhood. The strange displacement of 'home' to a place you talked and sang about all year and visited in the summer months. Leaving Ireland was the only choice that poor people like my parents had. I don't think my parents ever fully felt at home in London. Yes, they had plenty of Irish friends in Ealing. But they felt an anxiety, and I did too, about putting down roots in a place we were only visiting. "We are going home to Ireland this year. Are you?" was a question my school friends often asked about Ireland, even though they and I were born and bred in London. We lived in that space between. Catholic schools, churches and Irish pubs all fed the 'myth of return,' and it was powerful stuff.' [30] Whelan, now resident in the USA, hasn't ever returned. He has kept moving.

As I'm writing this there is footage on the BBC of Syrian refugees heading back through Europe. They are trying to get back home. They are returning. How many of them will get there I don't know, but whatever the numbers, in the case of immigrants, migrants and refugees, the actual return home is never as prevalent as the myth of return. Some people might well go back, those Syrian refugees walking their way back, for instance. Some might return but all live with the myth of it. I recall working with older Afro-Caribbean men in England in the 1990s who assured me, and themselves, that they were one day going

_____
30 Brian Whelan, *Myth of Return* (Roseberry Crest, 2010).

back. I don't know if they ever did. The young Irishwoman on the boat lived with the myth of return from the moment the boat set sail. The idea of going back quickly becoming as necessary a part of immigration as leaving in the first place. She never once thought, as she looked back from those railings, well, that's the end of that.

As immigrants in a British context the Irish are somewhat peculiar, somewhat singular, in that their country of origin is so close. Their home is nearby. It would still be wrong, though, to think that the idea of return, this myth, is predicated on the practicalities of going back. It is not about that at all. In fact the myth of return is not about going back, however much it is that idea it clearly represents, that it embodies. To think that it is about going back is to misunderstand immigration, migration, being a refugee. It is to misunderstand what it is the immigrant has done and is doing. The myth of return isn't about going back. Going home. The myth of return is instead about the opposite.

The myth of return, you see, is about the act of staying. Not only that, the myth of return is necessary for the act of staying.

The young woman on the boat, who ends up living in England for over forty years, never once admits she is staying. She never once confesses that she is there indefinitely. She doesn't admit this to anyone else and she doesn't admit it to herself. If the immigrant, or the migrant, or the refugee ever admits that this is long term, that this future is a perpetual one, they would be admitting more than they could bear. For the immigrant the future is always postponed. What they have instead is a temporary life. A temporary life, decade after decade. What they have is the myth of return. With this they are always going back. With this going back is always a possibility. Even when it isn't. So necessary is this myth of return, as necessary as still referring to the other country as home, that to challenge it makes no sense. The immigrant life becomes predicated on the premise that in some way it is taking place elsewhere.

Day-in, day-out existence, decade after decade, is happening here, in London, for instance, or Birmingham, or Manchester, but this is only temporary until it resumes again in Galway, or Cork, or Mayo. The Irish meet each other on English streets in English cities and it is all by way of reasserting that this is a shared construction, a temporary stopping. They give each other the myth that they will all one day return. That they will all go back. Nobody would dream of asking anybody else about the practicalities of return, about leaving life here, leaving children and houses and jobs. Nobody would point out that the Ireland remembered no longer exists, that it did not stop in time the way it stopped in their minds. Nobody would suggest that the myth of return is impractical. Why would they? For some, who have, for one reason or another, not been back, the myth is easier to maintain. They left a country they have only seen since in their memories, in a song, or a story. Those who do go back, those with children who return for those long summers, find they have to engage in clumsy mental gymnastics. They have the place they remember and the country they last saw a few months ago, when their children were running around Irish lanes and Irish streets. Somehow they have to balance that country they left, remake it in their minds. Strangely, they don't have to make it realistic, or make it coherent. It can embody all of the contradictions that immigration contains anyway. It doesn't have to make sense. That is irrelevant because the myth of return is just that. It is a myth. It is not important that it come true. It does not have to contain a travel itinerary. It just has to be there. It just has to exist. For the immigrant, the migrant, the refugee, it is only important that the myth of return is there. That is all.

Brian Whelan's family succumbed to the myth of return and went back when he was nine years old. It didn't work out. 'My father was forced to return to London to earn money. In the end we all had to go back to London. I suppose it strengthened the idea that return was impossible, or just a myth. But I think my parents were always mentally 'crossing the water' anyway. When my mother became a widow she thought about going home but even being the youngest of eleven children, and my father being the second youngest of eleven, there really wasn't anyone left in Ireland for her. It had all changed so much. The water between England and Ireland was a geographical space but what creeps up on everyone is the time spent away. You could say her boats just rotted away on the shore.'[31]

---

[31]   Ibid.

ALAN SUGAR

Long before society became an entrepreneurial competition immigrants knew they had to succeed. Long before Alan Sugar became our social barometer. There are different grades to this, as being an immigrant, or a migrant, or a refugee can, at times, constitute utterly different conditions. The refugee, for instance, can succeed by managing to stay alive. The refugee escapes war and killing and destruction. It is hard to be more successful than that. For the immigrant, the economic refugee, if you like, there is a different onus. Why come this far and still be poor? Of course, there is a great irony in this in that immigrants, migrants and refugees are all at the bottom of the economic pecking order. They might be told 'you can succeed here, this is a meritocracy'. But they aren't told anything about how uneven the playing field is. They soon realise. How could they not?

The young woman from the boat knows about this all along. She is aware that amongst the complications of immigration there is both resentment and expectation. The resentment is the fact that to those who have stayed, those you have left behind, you have said, 'this isn't good enough for me'. The implication, because they have stayed, is that they are saying, it is good enough for them. They watch you go and you feel, as you step onto the gangway, as if you are saying both those things to them. It's not good enough for me but it is good enough for you. Otherwise you'd be on this boat too. They resent you for that. They resent you for leaving. She knows that. She knows that resentment is there amongst the tears. Strangely, she also realises that there is an expectation too, especially because those who stay have only fanciful notions of what the other place is like. It is both a bitter, barren place and a place where the streets are paved with gold. 'Oh, Mary, this London's a wonderful sight. There's people here digging by day and by night. They don't dig for potatoes nor barley nor wheat. But there's gangs of them digging for gold in the street.'[32] Whatever about the immigrant knowing quickly the falsehood of these words immigration contains its own expectation. The expectation is that you have hardly left, have hardly sundered your mother's family, simply in order to exchange the poverty of Ireland for the poverty of England. You may have left, and immigrants do, for any number of reasons around a smothering, deadening social structure but economics plays a part whether you want it to or not. When you got on that boat you were supposed to be heading to a better life and for better read richer.

After living in rooms their first family home is a terraced council house a mere kick away from the football stadium. It is inner-city England at its most inner-city. There is a pub at the top of the road and a park where the children she watches closely can play. If she ever wishes she can walk in to the city

---

[32]   Percy French, 'The Mountains of Mourne', 1896.

centre in about fifteen minutes. The house is a two-up, two-down with a small, fenced yard. The neighbours are from Pakistan and her children play with children whose family are from the other side of the world. She doesn't know how she feels about telling people back home that she and her family are to be moved because the house is to be demolished in a slum clearance. They have work here and a home and possibilities. But their house is less than modest and they have six children and the council are moving them on. The next house, where they stay for over thirty years, is a little further out. The street is a little more English and on it she is a little more Irish. There is a bit more room and the garden is longer and more enclosed. They are not next to the football stadium now but they still hear the roar of the crowd and at night they can see the industrial brightness of the floodlights. They have moved ten minutes away. She knows this is still the heartland of working-class England. She knows too, as she looks around, that aesthetically she has traded down. She knows that visitors from Ireland are not likely to arrive here and be awed by the beauty of the place. She knows that where she lives is basic and functional. She knows these streets are hard and unforgiving. She knows too that being home in Ireland suggests things that might not be true. It suggests a level of comfort and prosperity that is not reflected by their status in the inner city. People back where she started might still have only a little but, in truth, she doesn't have a great deal more.

What she does have though is her children and what they have is a life in a much bigger place. A much bigger place physically and mentally. There are possibilities here that do not exist where she came from. Possibilities that exist because she emigrated, because she became an immigrant. Some of those are simply a matter of scale, belonging to the fact that England is so much bigger. She has never thought that part of becoming an immigrant was to better herself and she does not think it now. It was more about having a future or, at least, having a different one. What she does think, though, what she knows is that there is an onus on her immigration to have an aspect of success that she does not think it can contain. An immigrant, a migrant, a refugee does not look out from the inner-city streets of emigration and believe in Hollywood endings. She heard often in Ireland the idea of the 'returning Yank', a returning emigrant to America, both admired and resented. The emigrant to the UK does not carry quite the same connotations but she knows certain things are still expected of her. Of her family. When the streetlights shine in of a night she is not sure her house on this street can ever match those assumptions. She knows that, like so many here in England itself, that those at home have little knowledge of immigrant life. They cannot imagine, even from such an emigration-shaped country, what immigrant life is like. The streetlight shines in from streets they know nothing about. The streets tear and strain under lives they know little about. They cannot know how an immigrant succeeds or how an immigrant fails. How could they? She watches the streetlight, her husband on night shifts, and thinks that those at home don't even know what an English night is. Never mind how an Irishwoman negotiates it.

TOMMY ROBINSON

The irony is that it is those who have left their homeland that face the most hostility for being from their homeland. Prejudice against immigrants is mathematical. It is a dreary equation. One leads inexorably on to the other. Immigration equals prejudice. The immigrants get off the boat and prejudice has its excuse. Bigots and racists and flag wavers are never original. They may assume their resentments are unique, are specific, but they aren't. However much they feel they are harbingers of a bright new objection, of some kind of national renewal, they aren't. They are in a long, dreary line of stone throwers and pitchfork wavers, unable to comprehend that today isn't yesterday. 'Tomorrow is ours' is the battle cry of those who want tomorrow to sound just like some imaginary, golden, yesterday. They raise their flags and their flags flutter predictably in the wind. Their flags speak of a place that doesn't really exist. Their flags speak of a place they don't even really understand. What do they know of England, Billy Bragg sang, turning Kipling on his head, that only England know. Their flags say not so much this is us and this where we belong but this is us and it is not you. Their flags say turn back. Their flags say you do not belong. And yes, looking at those flags, in the face of those flags, the irony is that it is those who have left their homeland who face the most hostility for being from their homeland. Anti-Irish feeling doesn't really surface in Ireland. The Irish in Ireland only hear whispers of it. They even, scratching their own prejudices, get to express a chauvinistic anger on behalf of something they don't encounter. It is, instead, the ones they look down upon for leaving who know exactly what prejudice and bigotry is. It is the Irish immigrant who suffers from being Irish.

Anti-Irish prejudice may not be the most prevalent of prejudices now, I don't know, I'm not constructing a league table, but it is one of the oldest. It is traditional. The young Irish woman got off the boat vaguely aware, vaguely unaware, that there was hostility towards her simply because of where she was from but she didn't remain unaware for long. The Irish immigrant, in the prejudiced mind, committed the usual contradictory sins. She was both lazy and a job stealer. She was both stupid and cleverly cunning. She was both peculiarly Sacred and a cold killer. She was both a fixated mother and a drunk. She was both living in a house just like yours and bringing the neighbourhood down. She was both getting the best of everything and living in a way so basic you couldn't comprehend it. She was both your friendly neighbour and an unknowable stranger. She didn't remain unaware for long. The context of the 1970s and the 1980s was IRA violence and unemployment. When the IRA exploded bombs in the English city she was living in she knew anti-Irish sentiment then. When the industrial decimation of Margaret Thatcher's economic policies hit the inner-city areas she lived in she knew knee-jerk anti-immigrant sentiment then. That there was a context, though, doesn't really matter. The context often applies but it it is not as necessary to the equation as the simple fact of immigration itself. The flavour of the prejudice against her was anti-Irish but the core sentiment was unchanged. The fact was that people disliked her, resented her, despised her and intellectually alienated her because she was an immigrant. The existence of bigotry isn't a construct of the politically correct. It is part of an immigrant's existence.

What she does realise when the unfriendly stares move on, when the comments are made about somebody else, is that the bigot is still smiling from behind it all. She is aware, as the decades go by and the crude caricatures of the thick-Irish joke are suddenly deemed crass, as her Irishness is judged more and more acceptable, that none of this matters. Anti-Irish prejudice may now be just one of the oldest, it may no longer be one of the most prevalent, it may have even been replaced by its antithesis. Being Irish may now be a positive. It may now be a bright thing. It may now be a cool thing. It may now be a mist-soaked Celtic thing. People may now love to hear her Irish accent. They may now wish to visit the country she once trekked home to each summer with six kids in tow. But she knows, the immigrant knows, of course, more than anyone – it is still the same. The bigots have just moved on. They are merely focusing elsewhere. Their gaze, for now, is on someone else. In fact so complete, so complex, so unreflective does this apparent turnaround seem that it is bedevilled with its own contradictions. The far-right founder of the EDL, Tommy Robinson, aka Stephen Christopher Yaxley-Lennon, is the child of an Irish woman. He is the child of an immigrant. He is of the immigrants. He is from those who lived through the old prejudices. Whether he is in any way aware of this contradiction I have no idea. Anti-Irish prejudice, though, does not seem to have made an appearance amongst the Union-Jacked hordes he led against the 'Muslamic infidel.'[33] If the Irish are on the resentment list now they are way down it. Anne Marie Waters, an Irishwoman, was ultimately deemed too bigoted even for the role of UKIP leader. She is an immigrant. She is a Dublin-born immigrant to England who sees other immigrants as the threat. She has called for an end to all Muslim immigration. Somehow the contradictions inherent in this seem lost on her. Bigotry hasn't left, the woman from the boat realises, as someone smiles at her voice. It has only mutated. The Paddy has been replaced by the Muslim and the Pole. The thick Mick has been ousted by the dumb Romanian. The palimpsest of the savage IRA murderer in every Irishman has been superimposed by the ISIS bomber in every Muslim. They are out there still, the flag wavers and the definers of who belongs and who doesn't. They are still fighting the

---

[33] 'The Muslamic Infidel', YouTube, March 19th, 2011.

good fight. Prejudice now fixes its steely gaze on Eastern Europeans who are, in typical immigrant contradiction, stealing jobs we don't have and don't want to do. They are usurping us by living in houses we don't want to live in. They are taking over the country at the same time as having no commitment to it and sending all their money back home. Prejudice fixes its outrage on Muslims because they want to destroy our way of life. The fact that Islamic terrorists kill other Muslims way more than anyone else is, it appears, a contradiction too far to grasp for even those immersed in contradiction. Tommy and Anne Marie, for instance. How ironic that the great contradictions, the bigots, are undone by a simple contradiction, at the core of their own belief. The Irishwoman from the railings of the boat, an immigrant well-versed in the nature of contradiction, sees this more clearly than anyone.

JOHN BERGER

The host country, perhaps warped by a sense of superiority, believes immigration is all about the host country. England, besotted with notions of itself, either self-loathing or self-love or some hybrid of both, believes immigrants come to England out of some concentrated idea of what England represents. It is the land of endless opportunity or the land of the soft touch. It is the land of employment or generous welfare. It is the land all immigrants, migrants and refugees dream of. The world, in this version of the world, is made up of those who get to read *The Daily Mail*, *Good Morning Britain* dolefully playing in the background, Big Ben chiming, and those who want to. Again, because bigotry is as contradictory as the immigration it obsesses about, immigrants, migrants and refugees see England both as the land of their dreams and despise the place. They want nothing more than to be part of the fabric of British society. And they want nothing more than to destroy it. Immigrants, you see, they want it all. What the host country gets wrong though is that immigration is only about the host country in a minimal way. It is about it in a cold economic sense, as the geographical location where the employment is, or the housing, or the safety. But coming in out of the rain is about coming in out of the rain. It is only incidentally about the roof or the tent that keeps the rain out. Immigration, migration, becoming a refugee is about the country left. It is about leaving far more than it is about arriving. In *A Seventh Man*, a study of the migrant life published in 1975 but just as applicable now, John Berger wrote 'the well-fed are incapable of understanding the choices of the under-fed. The world has to be dismantled and re-assembled in order to be able to grasp, however clumsily, the experience of another.'

Immigration is about the culture of the country left behind. The young Irishwoman on the boat, looking back from those railings, knows she is looking back at a country that expected this of her all along. A country, she admits, that reared her for this all along. Ireland has been a country of emigration for a long while. Irish people are used to it as a social idea. There were vast numbers emigrating in the 1950s. There were vast numbers emigrating in the 1980s. There were vast numbers emigrating in the years after 2008. There is hardly an Irish family that does not have some association with emigration. The President, Michael D. Higgins, speaks often of his own sisters and their immigrant lives in England. There might be complex issues, distorted psychologies about how Ireland deals with this emigration. The way it both condemns and resents it. The way those who stay, who do not emigrate, feel both inferior and superior to those who do. But the point is that emigration from Ireland, becoming an Irish immigrant, says far, far more about Ireland than it ever does about the country the emigrant ends up in. The leaving of Ireland is about Ireland. The young woman on the boat does not lean against those railings and look out at the coast she is sailing to. She looks back. She looks back because the emigration she is undertaking is because of the country she sees receding behind her. Immigrants, to put it coarsely, are always running away from something more than they are running towards something. Of course they have to arrive somewhere but the psychology of emigration is predicated upon the point of departure far more than it is the place of arrival. The mathematics of emigration is that some people leave so that some people can stay. The politics is that the same people leave so that the same people stay. The point is that this all to do, in this instance, with Ireland and not with England. England isn't the cause of Irish emigration or, if it is, it is only minimally compared to Ireland itself. The host country has to accept, however insulting it might seem, that immigrants don't come for the host country at all. They come for the leaving of their own.

Alan Kurdî didn't become a refugee because of the countries that are associated with his death. Alan Kurdî didn't drown in the Mediterranean because of Turkey or Greece or Canada, all countries his family either fled to or wanted to get to. Some of those countries may well look bleak in the way that they treated Alan Kurdî's people or treated refugees in general but they remain secondary in the story of his becoming a refugee. Alan Kurdî drowned because of what was happening in his home country of Syria. In the case of migrants and refugees the role of the host country, the destination, is even less pronounced than it is in the Irish case. Immigration is integral to the modern history of Irish society. Becoming a refugee is integral to the history of the last number of global decades. Becoming a citizen of that made-up country, the twenty-first-largest State in the world, is integral to that of immigrants, migrants and refugees. It is integral because of where they are leaving, not because of the qualities of the made-up country. Somalians migrate because of the collapse of anything approaching a State in their own country. Jewish refugees escape out of Germany in the 1930s because of Nazi control of their State. Syrians flee Syria because of war and destruction in Syria. Refugees flood across the Balkan mountains in the 1990s because of the implosion of their own countries. Libyans seek asylum in Europe because of their State's disintegration. The people who wend their way, in a long snaking line, on a poster behind Nigel Farage don't do so because Nigel is up ahead. They do so because of what is behind them. Nigel, perhaps warped by a sense of superiority, doesn't understand that, but then asking Nigel Farage to understand immigration is like asking Donald Trump to understand dignity. It would be a sign of not taking our subject matter seriously.

She has many good things to say about the city she ended up in. The city where she spent nearly four decades of her life. The city where her six children were born. The city her children sound like. She has many good things to say about all of the Irish she knew there, about the Emerald Club and the Sunday afternoons. She has many good things to say about those from every county of Ireland she met there, that she would never have encountered if she'd stayed at home. She has many good things to say about the life she found and made and built in that city. She has many good things to say about the English, even if some could see no further than her being Irish, and some could not help but watch her warily as she cleaned their houses. She has many good things to say about those other immigrants she met on those inner-city streets. She has many fond memories of the streetlight shining in through the window. She has good things to say. But she cannot say that her becoming an Irish immigrant had anything to do with England. She cannot say it had anything to do with England at all.

NIGEL FARAGE

Immigration is a victory of the imagination. The young woman looking back from the boat came from a line of people who, for years, had followed paths of internal migration. Landless, they crossed county lines, to work fields belonging to someone else. They drifted from rural to urban, chasing accommodation and employment. They led migrant lives inside their own country. They became used to impermanence. Indeed, impermanence became their accepted understanding of life. She grew up with this. She grew up around it. She knew the mentality of the migrant and knew no other. In Ireland she was to realise that whole swathes of the population knew this mentality too. They may have been the urban poor or the rurally impoverished, they may not have chased settlement the way her people did, but they were from the same world. In this life economic hardship was a given, seasonal unemployment a fact, social advancement a whisper from somebody else's life. That is not to say that these people weren't joyous or exuberant. It is not to suggest that they didn't know the importance of having a bloody good laugh. They did. Such people, in fact, were more attached to the ludic than others because sometimes it was all they had. What they did not have, though, was luxury or security or any great amount of comfort. What they did not have was the belief that poverty was elsewhere or happening to somebody else. They were part of the Nation-State. Perhaps, nearer to the essence of it than most. Perhaps, more typically Irish than those who knew nothing of working somebody else's fields. Indeed, at times, it seemed that their Irishness and their attachment to it was about all they had. Yet, if they were stakeholders in the country, their stake was bent in the wind. They were part of the Nation-State. But only just.

The young woman knew little about the country she was heading to. She knew Britain was there, at the end of the docks, but that was about all. Of the city she would live in she knew less. She had never stepped foot in it, the place she would live in for over forty years, until she stepped foot in it. She had come out of a people who were expected to emigrate, for whom emigration was seen as a natural occurrence. She did have that. She did have emigration as a tradition. What she did not have was any evidence of what it would be like. She did not have any knowledge of where she was going. She only had her imagination. Immigrants and migrants and refugees are equipped with many things. Desperation and fright would be high on the list, but they also have imagination. They have to imagine that there is a better life possible for them. They have no, or little, evidence to support this, but they imagine it all the same. They imagine from far worse places than the young woman on the boat has known. She knows stultifying poverty and economic stagnation. She knows a life without possibility. She knows that her life is set in a drab, rigged groove, unless she gets on the boat. She does not know, though, a rifle butt pushing her on. She does not know the terror of barbed wire or incipient violence. She has not seen her country disappear into factional quarters of conflict. She hasn't fled because she feared being killed. Like those who did though, like those who do, she has imagined a life and that imagined life was all she had. When she got on the boat she was committing an act of imagination.

In this strange age of ours we celebrate things we once thought were the opposite of positives. We embrace them. So it is that the entrepreneurial spirit is used as a cover for human qualities we once opposed. We applaud the vain and the selfish. *The Apprentice* and *Dragon's Den* inculcate an attitude of self-advancement at any cost and millions are encouraged to nurture that dream. Knowing the cost of everything and the value of nothing is now a virtue. The public good is an anathema because private advancement is where we're at. In this set of values you should only pull someone from the water if you've done a full cost-benefit analysis. Fittingly enough, in this upside-down world, we then dismiss the truest entrepreneurs amongst us. Somehow those who have crossed continents with nothing more than their imaginings of what life might be are not celebrated. Somehow those who have been set the most impossible tasks and overcome them are not embraced. The refugee, with such a wealth of innovation that they were able to get as far as here, is not welcomed with open arms. The migrant, who insists that this job will be the one that gets them there, is not applauded. The immigrant, with little but the ability and fortitude to imagine the future, is not rewarded. So lost in spite, for instance, was Nigel Farage that he couldn't see that the snaking line behind him was spilling from a reservoir of imaginative entrepreneurs who, if they'd had Nigel's advantages, would surely have done more than end up standing woefully in front of a pastiche of Nazi propaganda. Nigel's entrepreneurial politics appear to stem from a place of such intellectual poverty it is hard to imagine him enduring what those behind him quite clearly have. It is hard to imagine his imagination.

He is not alone though. There is a poverty of thought around immigrants and migrants and refugees and it is all loaded on one side. The immigrants themselves, getting off the night ferry from all of the counties of Ireland, had suitcases wrapped in string. They had little and what they mainly had knowledge of was poverty. They knew poverty as a fact of daily Irish life. The migrants come and do work no one else will entertain. They do that because they have so little to begin with that they will pick vegetables, or remove asbestos, or any other job that can't be filled. The refugees have so little they might only possess what they stand up in. They have such poverty that they come from places that might not exist any longer. They only want to be pulled out of the water. What they all have, though, what they all possess is imagination enough to envisage a life they cannot see. They wend their way behind Nigel and their imagination is in front of them. By contrast Nigel, and all his weary companions, have such a dearth of imaginative qualities that they do not even see men, women and children. They have such a poverty that they can only brutalise with vocabulary the humanity that appears before them. Where some see people they see only immigrants and migrants and refugees and the words in their mouths are harsh because they do not have the mental vocabulary for them not to be. Their words are meant to demean. It is as if they are the only words they have. They only possess enough imagination to call someone an immigrant and in their imagination that is as low as you can go.

ALAN KURDÎ

They keep coming. It is true what the reactionaries and the racists say. The immigrants just keep coming. The atavistic nature of bigotry is only matched by the atavistic nature of immigration. The science of immigration is as certain as the science of gravity. Immigration is a part of what human beings do. In this way there is even something Sisyphean about the anti-immigrant brigade. About, say, Trump and his wall. It won't work and it's foolish. It's meaningless. Of course that's not really the point. The point is the gesture. Like a Britain First march it is not really designed to work. Those marching beneath the theatre of Union Jacks do not really imagine they are taking back the streets, they don't really believe they're about to take back the country they think they've lost. Even the racists know the immigrants will just keep on coming.

Anti-immigration groups come in many guises now and use that cause as an umbrella for many others. In the UK and Ireland alone there is UKIP, the EDL, Pegida, the Immigration Control Platform, Britain First, oh and so many splinter groups I've grown weary just writing them down. There used to be an old Brendan Behan's joke that the first item on the meeting of any Irish Republican organisation was, 'when's the split?' That joke's on the racists and bigots now. Indeed, they froth and bubble with so much hatred it is not hard to imagine that they don't easily coalesce. Trump's election, it is said, has legitimised these people but I'm not sure how convincing that is. The young woman on the boat has so much more intellectual solidity, simply by virtue of her actions, that it is hard to see how she could ever be outflanked by an argument that relies on Donald Trump. Bigotry is internally incoherent. That it is a home for the emotionally stagnant and the intellectually inadequate seems self-evident. This is not a complex argument. Immigration makes sense in every way. It makes sense economically, culturally and socially. An immigrant-enriched society is an enriched society. Immigration is not only inevitable, it is a boon. Some of the reactionaries even admit this. They talk about controlled immigration, about how important it is to control their own borders. This too is incoherent. Not just for the racists who dream of some kind of white, Christian-only immigration but for the respectable prejudices embodied by, for instance, UKIP. Likewise Ireland's minuscule Immigration Control Platform group even states on its own website that 'no one who holds views of racial superiority is welcome in the group' despite having a raison d'être based on that very thing. Immigration is already a controlled thing. It controls itself. The young woman on the boat joined thousands of others on the boat because there was no employment in Ireland and there was lots of employment in Britain. The incoherence of deriding some people as only economic refugees, merely economic migrants, is a contradiction. Not only is poverty as much about politics as war and conflict but all immigration is economic. We are back again with the misguided idea that emigration to England is about England. The young woman does not leave the rolling hills and quiet byways of Cork for the aesthetic pleasures of the industrial English Midlands. She doesn't leave the warmth and readiness of her family for the distant regard of strangers. She doesn't leave a culture she is part of for a culture she doesn't understand. In 1989 the right-wing political scientist, Francis Fukuyama, published an essay called 'The End of History?'. It was a statement that all was settled now, that there were no more competing ideologies, that things were as they were because that was how they should be. It is a Bertie Wooster version of reality. God is in his heaven and all's right with the world. Unfortunately for Fukuyama it also follows the Wodehouse dictum that there are two ways of looking at life: 'making a sort of musical comedy without music and ignoring real life altogether; the other is going right deep down into life and not caring a damn.'[34] The simple passage of time has proven that whilst Fukuyama may have thought he was going deep down into life and bringing back incontrovertible truths he was actually writing a musical comedy without the music. Political systems and human societies continue to be unstable and unpredictable. The idea that human history is settled is as ludicrous now as it was then. Immigrants, migrants and refugees, economic or otherwise, know this more than anybody else. They keep on coming, they keep on appearing, they keep crossing the sea. The sun will go down and the racists will go to bed and there will still be immigrants. That can't be debated as good or bad. It just is.

Somewhere now there is a young woman on a boat. She is looking back from the railings. It is easy to have a picture of her in your mind but she is real too. She is flesh

---

[34] P.G. Wodehouse, *Performing Flea* (Herbert Jenkins, 1953).

and blood. I'm not sure what she is leaving, whether she is reluctantly forced out by poverty or gratefully escaping bloodshed. I don't know or have any definite way of knowing. I know she is there though. I know she is real. We only have Alan Kurdî from a photograph but I know he is real too. I know these are flesh and blood people. People you could reach out and touch. People whose hand you could grasp, that you could pull from the water. That there are stresses and strains from immigration is obvious. Immigrants, migrants and refugees also know that more than anybody else, because they live completely in the places where it occurs. The symbolism of that is not irrelevant. So much of what is written and said and opined about immigrants and migrants and refugees is not written or said by immigrants or migrants or refugees. So much of the discourse around immigration is by those who are not immigrants. Indeed so much of what is said about them is never even heard by them. They have their heads down, hurrying by, making stretched ends meet. In effect the discussion, if it can be called that, about and around immigration, is only ever half a discussion. The young woman on the boat, the young woman then and the young woman now, is not taking part in the discussion. She, of course, hears things. She knows the hostility and the resentment. She hears the whispers. She hasn't come this far, though, to stop and listen to that. She is not getting to the end of that exhausting line and stopping to hear what Nigel has to say. Why would she bother?

They keep coming. Even as I write this, even as you read it, there will be another small boy like Alan Kurdî making his way across land and water. We can't see or hear him yet but we know he is there. We can't ever hear from Alan Kurdî himself though. We will never hear his voice. We can't ever hear what that small boy might have said. We only know that he was more than just a photograph, more than just an image. We know that he was a flesh and blood boy. We know if we'd seen him in that water what we would have done. We know we would have reached out and pulled him in. We would have taken him from the water. We know that. We know that if we could have held him in our arms we would have.

POSTSCRIPT: ZHAO LIUTAO

On a wet January evening in 2002, Ireland is in the midst of an unprecedented economic boom. It is the days of the so-called Celtic Tiger. Such is the tenor of the times that the Taoiseach Bertie Ahern would state as late as 2006, with his own inimitable use of the English language, that the 'boom times are getting even more boomer.'[35] In this boom-time Ireland some young people are walking home through the streets of the capital city, Dublin. They are a group of Chinese people who are all living in the city. It is a typically wet Irish evening. Before they get home they are shouted at and then set upon by a gang of local youths. One of the group, a man called Zhao Liutao, is hit over the head with an iron bar and dies three days later of his injuries. It is described as Ireland's 'first racially motivated murder'.[36]

---

[35] *The Irish Times*, 14th July, 2006.
[36] *BBC News* website, 11th February, 2002.

In newspaper photographs of one of the men subsequently found guilty of Zhao Liutao's murder, a young man is walking handcuffed into the court. He is looking warily at the camera. He is wearing a short-sleeved t-shirt. On his right forearm there is a clearly visible tattoo. It is of a red devil holding a spear. Across the body of the devil there is the green, white and gold of the Irish national flag. Zhao Liutao, a migrant student, had been in Ireland for little more than a couple of months. His brother came over to Ireland for the inquest into Zhao's death and stated that Zhao's plan was to return to China that summer.[37]

In 2018 the European Network against Racism in Ireland reported 'an alarming growth in racist hate crimes.'[38] These crimes ranged from physical and sexual assault through to online abuse. If even the Irish, if even the people the young woman on the boat came from, are anti-immigrant

---

[37] *Irish Independent*, 1st February, 2002

[38] *ENR Ireland*, 2018.

and anti-migrant and anti-refugee, is history silent? If even the Irish, who in decades, for instance, like the 1950s, the 1980s and the 2010s, emigrated in huge numbers, became, in effect, immigrants and migrants and refugees, are prejudiced, are racist, are bigots, what is there to say? If even the Irish produce a man who will tattoo himself with his national flag and kill someone else for being from somewhere else? Or, at least, look as if they might be? Well for Alan Kurdî, for Zhao Liutao, for the young woman standing by the railings of the boat one thing we can do, one thing we can all easily do, is listen very, very carefully to the words spoken by Nigel Farage, Donald Trump or Boris Johnson. We can listen to them and imagine what they sound like, what they mean, to an immigrant or a migrant or a refugee walking home late at night. The comedian Stewart Lee, who has performed an entire sketch on the perils of language, has traded laughs for showing just how important, how real, such words are. He has been explicit about the truth that lies beyond the laughs. 'The problem is 84 per cent of people apparently, of the public, think that political correctness has gone mad. Now, I don't know if it has. People still get killed, don't they, for being the wrong colour or the wrong sexuality or whatever. And what is political correctness? It's an often-clumsy negotiation towards a kind of formally inclusive language. And there's all sorts of problems with it but it's better than what we had before.'[39]

The young woman in this book is a real person. A flesh-and-blood person. The immigrant label is one used to describe her, to label her, to demean her. It would be the same if she was a migrant or a refugee which, of course, in a way she is. All immigrants are migrants because psychologically their state is only ever temporary. 'So we live here, forever taking leave.' [40] They are refugees too, economic refugees if nothing else. Alan

39 Stewart Lee, *How I Escaped My Certain Fate* (Faber, 2010).
40 Rainer Maria Rilke, *The Duino Elegies*, 1923.

Kurdî was a real person too. Zhao Liutao was a real person. We would put out our hands to help them if we could. To pull them from the water or prevent that killing blow. But we have to know that there are some people who wouldn't. Who will never see beyond immigrant, migrant or refugee when they see the young woman on the boat or Alan Kurdî or Zhao Liutao. This book has to recognise that. We have to recognise those people are there. We have to recognise, too, that they are not all sporting nationalistic tattoos on their forearms. We have to recognise that some of them are wearing suits and that when they speak they speak not the shouted words of a late night attack but the words of power and privilege.

My deepest thanks to Amira Ghanim, Alex Wylie and Todd Swift at Eyewear/Black Spring Press Group. My love to my brother and sisters who walked the same streets. My everything to Kitty and the kids. And, mostly, my love and unending admiration to my mother, the immigrant woman. This book is because of her.